MW01259197

FISHING LIMESTONE STREAMS

FISHING LIMESTONE STREAMS

A Complete Guide to Fishing
These Unique Waters

Charles Meck

THE LYONS PRESS
Guilford, Connecticut
An imprint of The Globe Pequot Press

The Lyons Press is an imprint of The Globe Pequot Press.

10   9   8   7   6   5   4   3   2   1

Printed in the United States of America

Designed by Maggie Peterson

Library of Congress Cataloging-in-Publication Data

Meck, Charles R.
  Fishing limestone streams : a complete guide to fishing this
unique riverine environment /
Charles Meck.
    p.   cm.
ISBN 1-59228-614-3 (trade cloth)
  1. Trout fishing.   2. Fly fishing.   I. Title.
  SH687.M343 2005
  799.17'57--dc22

                                                        2004065013

DEDICATION

Lieutenant Michael Adams

Mike Adams was the Cadet-in-Charge of the Cadet Fly Fishing Club at the United States Military Academy from June 1999 until his commissioning as a second lieutenant in the Army, in June 2002. While at West Point, Mike was a leader and mentor, and an ambassador of fly fishing. Prior to Mike's arrival at West Point, the fly-fishing club drifted from year to year without continuity. He set a new course for the club: To educate, train, and inspire the future leaders of this nation through fly fishing. He established a program to focus on fly-fishing techniques, crafts (fly tying and rod building), and conservation.

Left to right: Mike Adams, the author, Ryan Zimmerman, and Doug Matty fishing Spruce Creek in May 2002.

Mike was a fly fisher since his childhood and possessed both a wealth of practical knowledge and a passion for the sport. With Mike on board, the West Point club began to progress. Membership climbed from six to over sixty active members. The officer and non-commissioned officer cadre that provides institutional support for the club grew from a single faculty sponsor to a total of ten officers, non-commissioned officers, and civilians.

In May 2002, Academy faculty member Major Douglas Matty asked me if I would host two cadets as a reward for their great service to the fly-fishing club. Mike Adams, fellow cadet Ryan Zimmerman, and Major Matty fished with me on the Spruce Creek Rod and Gun Club waters in central Pennsylvania for an entire weekend. They caught more than fifty trout during those two days. Some of those trout weighed more than four pounds.

I'll never forget how excited Mike was when he landed his last and best trout. He ran up to me and said, "Sir, I just landed the biggest trout I've ever caught." He guessed it was at least 24 inches long.

Mike Adams' life and love of fly fishing were cut short in Iraq on March 16, 2004. He was riding in a tank with the Third Armored Cavalry Regiment, providing an escort for a convoy, when an automobile crashed into his tank and killed him. He had one week to go before he finished his tour of duty.

I will always remember Mike, his intense interest in fly fishing, and his keen respect for others. We owe a debt of gratitude to him and all those who serve to protect us so we can enjoy the things we like to do without fear, including fishing.

CONTENTS

MAPS

TABLES

ACKNOWLEDGMENTS

The manuscript for this book was due to the publisher by September 1, 2004. On May 13, less than four months before the final deadline, I fell off a ladder and broke my left arm—my casting arm. I soon had surgery and the doctor placed four pins into the bone to hold it together while it healed. For the next eight weeks I had to wear a steel brace that held those pins in place. It was quite painful, and it wasn't pretty. Then in late July I had the pins removed early because they became infected. But I still couldn't fish, and my wife, Shirley, had to drive me to most of the limestone streams so I could do the necessary on-site research. Then, on August 10, Shirley broke her leg. She couldn't drive. I would say it was all a comedy of errors, but I can't bring myself to laugh at the broken bones.

Thus, was it not for the people I mention here, this book could never have been written. Thanks to all of you.

Bill Gamber of Lancaster, Pennsylvania, arranged a meeting for me so I could interview Bob Kutz and Greg Wilson of the Donegal Chapter of Trout Unlimited. Bill is a tremendous fly fisher and an even greater person.

Kurt Thomas' expertise as a guide provided me with a good deal of insight into various limestone streams. He's one of the top guides I have seen in my fifty years of fly fishing.

Mike Heck, a guide on south-central Pennsylvania streams, and Brad Etchberger accompanied me on Big Spring Creek near Newville.

Dave Herold, another great fly fisher, fished with me on Monocacy Creek in Bethlehem.

I was supposed to meet Andy Leitzinger and fish Valley Creek in Valley Forge with him. My wife broke her leg the day before that meeting, however, so I had to interview Andy by telephone. No matter. His help was invaluable.

Mark Sturtevant and Mike Saylor helped me immeasurably on Falling Spring Branch in Pennsylvania and Beaver Creek in Maryland.

Bob Toolan let me hang around while he guided his friend, Bill King, on Cedar Creek and Saucon Creek, as I watched.

Joe DeMarkis gave the time to Bob and Bill to work with me; Joe owns Old Lehigh Outfitters in Bethlehem, Pennsylvania, and Bob is one of his guides.

I could not have written about the limestone streams of Virginia without the help of Colby and Brian Trow.

In addition, I was greatly helped by my interviews with Bob Cramer, a fantastic guide who taught me all about Mossy Creek in Virginia.

Dr. William Sharpe of the Pennsylvania State University gave me many good editorial suggestions.

Thanks to all of you and many others for your support and help.

INTRODUCTION

Almost forty years ago, Barry Beck and Vince Marinaro invited me to Falling Spring Branch, a small, cold, clear limestone stream in south-central Pennsylvania, to see a tiny mayfly hatch at the height of the summer. Both of these men by that time were true fly-fishing experts: Barry was an upcoming notable, and of course Vince was well known for his books, *In the Ring of the Rise*, and, *A Modern Dry-Fly Code*. I was in total awe of these two professionals that day and sat back to watch both of them fish.

We hit a famous, albeit tiny hatch that day; the very first hatch I ever watched, in fact. Tricos by the thousands first appeared as duns, and then a few minutes later moved back over the water in close formation in their typical ritual as mating male and female spinners. All of these intricacies were new for me that day: the hatch; the clear, cool water; and two masters trying to convince the trout that the fly floating over them was a real mayfly.

I watched and waited for Vince to catch his first trout. And I waited. And waited. I watched the master for maybe an hour cast over one rising trout after another without any success. I did not realize that this same hatch had appeared every morning for the past two months. Nor did I know that these trout had been fished over with similar patterns for more than two months by many other frustrated anglers. These were possibly the most wizened trout I had yet seen.

By 9 A.M., the spinner fall was at its zenith and Vince continued to fish over maybe twenty trout now feeding on those tiny, spent Trico spinners. Fish fed everywhere—in front of Vince, to his side, and even behind him.

The author with a brown trout on Falling Spring Branch, where Vince Marinaro once met his match.

They fed as close as ten feet from him. But he couldn't buy a strike if his life and reputation depended on it.

"Tell the trout who you are, Vince," Barry called out, with a smile, while standing on the high bank above.

Vince mumbled a bit, nothing that was audible to me, and he continued to fish. For more than an hour I just sat back on that high bank overlooking this fertile limestone stream and kept my eyes peeled, and kept quiet. I figured that if Vince Marinaro couldn't catch any trout I had no chance in hell of catching one myself.

Those trout had probably inspected more than two hundred patterns presented to them in the past two months that the hatch had appeared. Watching an expert like Vince get stymied let me know that this was no easy game but required much observation and thought.

Although I never once cast a fly that day, that hatch and that small limestone stream have remained a clear picture in my memory for almost forty years. I have returned to that same spot on Falling Spring Branch

The Heritage Angling area of Falling Spring Branch. Such waters often call for long, fine leaders and very small flies.

many times since and experienced that same frustration that Vince Marinaro did that day long ago.

That frustration of fishing over highly selective trout is very common on many of the heavier fished limestone streams no matter where they flow. These fertile waters hold plenty of hatches and trout, and consequently draw intense fishing pressure. Angling crowds produce trout that are extremely difficult to catch. But this book, *Fishing Limestone Streams*, will help you be successful on these streams by examining what makes limestone streams so special, what kind of insects can be found in them, and what tactics and fly patterns will make you successful.

Limestone streams are unique environments. They differ greatly from freestone streams. I'll discuss this in detail in chapter 1.

What are some of the better limestone streams in the East? You'll find a discussion of many of these in chapters 2 and 3. In many cases, I have looked at local limestone streams through the eyes of an accomplished fishing guide who has spent much more time on the stream than I have.

Most of our great limestone streams harbor more than just the Trico hatch. Such rich waters also hold good numbers of mayflies like Little Blue-Winged Olive Duns, Sulphurs, Green Drakes, and more. But what is out of sight on these streams is often as important as what you see on the surface: Crayfish, scuds, and sow bugs often proliferate in these waters. We'll take a detailed look at the most common trout food on these streams in chapter 4.

Fishing many of these limestone waters like Falling Spring Branch often calls for some special tactics. Long, very fine leaders and small flies, up to size 22, are required. In my time fishing in Pennsylvania, I've met a number of veteran anglers and guides who've taught me a thing or two about limestone tactics that only years of fishing taught them. In chapter 5 I'll clue you in on all the essential nuances and special tactics I've learned.

A lot of the fly patterns that anglers cast on limestone waters were developed for specific streams. For example, my friend Al Miller probably

Do limestones hold big fish? You bet. Here, the author's son, Bryan Meck, shows off a big brown from a favorite Pennsylvania stream.

fishes the Little Lehigh a hundred days a year, and there he came up with his own specific pattern: Al's Rat, a top producer on that stream. In chapter 6, you'll find many effective limestone patterns described in detail. A good number of them were developed by professional guides, and all of them have worked for me at one time or another on various streams.

Finally, in chapter 7 I'll discuss what the future holds for limestone streams in the East. Unfortunately, it isn't all bright. Problems like pollution, sedimentation, and privatization top the list of concerns. We must take action to preserve what public waters are left and repair those in trouble.

But there's a lot of great fishing out there in Pennsylvania, and in Maryland and Virginia, too. I hope *Fishing Limestone Streams* will help take you to it.

FISHING LIMESTONE STREAMS

1

The Nature of Limestone Streams

Limestone streams are formed by water flowing through limestone and dolomite bedrock. In the eastern United States, a great number of these streams are found in central Pennsylvania, Maryland, and northern Virginia (see the maps at the end of the chapter). As these waters flow through this bedrock they dissolve calcium carbonate from the rock which raises the pH or alkalinity of the water. A pH of 7 is neutral. A pH near 8 is not unusual on limestone waters.

There are several types of limestone waters. First is the classic limestone stream that emerges as a pool or spring. Penns Creek, Boiling Spring Run, Falling Spring Branch, Spruce Creek, and countless others begin their journey from a huge spring. Second, some so-called limestone streams begin as freestone streams and then receive a huge influx of limestone water from a major tributary. The lower Bald Eagle Creek after Spring Creek enters is an example of this type of limestone stream. Third, some streams—usually larger waters—are mainly freestone in nature but are influenced by limestone springs entering them. The Juniata River, the Little Juniata River, the Frankstown Branch of the Juniata River in central Pennsylvania, and the North River in Virginia are examples of this type of water. Fourth, many limestone waters begin as freestone streams in their upper, mountainous origin. They flow a few miles as a freestone stream, flow across limestone formations as they go underground, and then re-emerge as a limestone stream. Honey Creek in south-central Pennsylvania and Long Run in central Pennsylvania begin like this.

Many limestone streams exhibit a combination of one, two, or three of the types. Look at Spruce Creek in central Pennsylvania. Spruce Creek begins as a collection of several unnamed freestone streams that go underground. Then the limestone section of Spruce Creek erupts as a spring-fed pool near Rock Springs. Several miles downstream, just below Baileyville, dozens of additional springs enter the main stem.

Freestone streams usually flow through sandstone, shale, or crystalline rocks. Many freestone waters that are adversely affected by acid rains often maintain a pH of much less than 7 in the spring. Moreover, some freestone streams located on ridges and impacted by acid rains register a pH near or lower than 5 in March and April. These lower pHs don't bode well for trout. Because of their alkalinity limestone streams have a natural buffer against acid rains.

I said earlier that limestone streams often begin with a huge influx of water from a large spring. The volume of springs in the East ranges as high

The classic limestone streams originate from a spring, emerging as a large pool, such as Falling Spring Branch.

as 18,000 gallons per minute (gpm). "First-magnitude" streams are considered those with a flow higher than 45,000 gpm. Pennsylvania has at least eleven springs that flow with more than 6,000 gpm. These are considered "second magnitude" springs, and are most often located in karst limestone valleys rather than mountains where most freestone streams originate. Karst regions are characterized by limestone bedrock with large sinkholes, disappearing streams, limestone caverns, and great springs discharging large volumes of 50-degree water year-round.

Water in limestone streams is usually colder, has fewer species of fish, holds more invertebrates, and hosts a higher concentration of aquatic plants than do freestone streams of the same volume. The temperature of the water coming through these large springs is usually quite close to the mean air temperature in the region (about 50 degrees in the mid-Atlantic region). Because these limestone waters have consistently colder temperatures than most freestones, trout and a few species of minnows and suckers might be the only inhabitants of this colder water. But those freestone streams that fluctuate more in temperature and are warmer will often harbor additional fish species that prefer warmer water. Where a cold limestone stream might hold only a handful of fish species, warmer freestone water might harbor five, ten, or more different species.

Many limestone waters characteristically submerge for part of their journey downstream. Some do this for just a short distance, others do it for miles, but in all cases these waters are cooler from their time underground. In late summer, when stream flows are low, all or much of the water in some limestone streams may disappear underground, such as with Honey, Sinking, Big Fishing, Little Bushkill, and Pine Creeks and Long Run.

The location of limestone streams is both a blessing and a bane. It's a blessing because these streams are easy to access, often flow slowly, and begin with a cold spring. But it's also a curse because they often flow through heavily farmed areas. Cultivated farmlands often use every inch of fertile land right up to the stream bank. This usually leads to heavy sedimentation and some runoff that in turn lowers the number of insects and fish in the stream.

Some limestone streams begin as freestone waters; Little Fishing Creek flows from this small freestone that holds numerous brook trout.

Limestone streams normally run cooler than freestones in the summer. Warmer freestone streams see lower water flows in the summer. Often summer temperatures on a freestone can rise into the high 70s or low 80s whereas its limestone counterpart, cooled by underground water sources, may only rise into the 60s.

Winter is another story. At that time of year many freestone streams freeze over. Many limestone streams, however, hold a higher temperature relative to freestone ones and often they don't freeze over, allowing for insect growth and development. You'll often find numerous midwinter midge hatches on the relatively open waters of limestone streams.

Ultimately, limestones provide better forage for trout and a higher concentration of insects (mainly mayflies and caddisflies) than do freestone streams of the same size because of their higher alkalinity, less extreme temperatures, and moderate changes in flows. Herein is the value of these streams to the fly fisher (and a reason for this book): Limestones are natural trout havens. You guarantee yourself a maximization of "trout time" when you fish them.

Limestones can also influence other waters. Here, a cool limestone tributary (foreground) enters the Juniata River at Frankstown.

TABLE 1: COMPARISON OF LIMESTONE
AND FREESTONE STREAM FEATURES

Limestone	Freestone
Associated with limestone and dolomite bedrock	Associated with sandstone, shale, and crystalline rocks
Usually begins in a valley	Usually begins in a mountain
Usually colder in the summer	Often warmer in the summer
Usually higher flow in the summer	The water flow and the stream temperature can vary year-long
More regulated stream flow throughout the year	More affected by acid rains
Better midwinter midge hatches	Streams often freeze over in the winter
Often holds fewer species of fish	More diversity of fishes
More sedimentation due to farming	Lower pH and less alkalinity
Often begins with a large spring	Originates as ground water
Often flows underground for part of its journey and/or part of the year	Flows above ground for entire journey
More aquatic plants	
More insect species	

THE IMPORTANCE OF LIMESTONE STREAMS

A limestone stream's high alkalinity acts as a buffer against the acid rains so common in the East. This is crucial to trout fishing.

Consider Linn Run, a freestone stream flowing northwest off the Allegheny Plateau. It enters the Loyalhanna Creek near Ligonier, Pennsylvania. In March, that stream often records a pH in the low 5s or even in the high 4s. Just forty air miles to the east flows a limestone stream called Yellow Creek, in Bedford County. At the same time that Linn Run flows with a pH of 5 or lower, Yellow records a pH well above 7. How does a lower pH affect stream conditions? First, fewer aquatic insects, especially mayflies, can survive highly acidic conditions. Second, this high acidity also affects trout, especially their ability to regulate body salts and few can survive for an extended time in a low pH environment.

Another highly important aspect of limestone streams and limestone springs entering larger rivers is that they cool the water downriver considerably. This creates opportunities that would otherwise not exist, because

Many limestone streams, like Half Moon Creek, pictured here, flow underground for part of their journey during low-water conditions.

on those days when the water warms considerably, trout seek out these cooler, spring-fed waters. Locate the cool water and you've found the fish.

If I live to be a hundred I'll still remember that day that Jim Ravasio asked me to guide him and a doctor friend, Bob Budd, in central Pennsylvania. That day in late July the air temperature rose to nearly 100 degrees. The humidity also was unbearably high. It was a totally intolerable day to fly fish. We spent the entire morning traveling from one freestone stream to another searching for cool water. The last freestone stream we fished was Wallace Run, a small mountain stream flowing down from the Allegheny Plateau. When we arrived at the stream we were greeted with a bare trickle of water. In an entire morning and early afternoon of fly fishing we caught a total of two trout. Finally, I'd had it.

We headed to the Little Juniata River twenty-five miles to the southwest. The "LJ" is a fairly large river, and we planned to fish it about five miles below Tyrone. In that area the river gets a cool surge of water from four separate, fairly large limestone streams and springs. We fished just

Freestone water flow fluctuates much more than limestone flow, especially in summer, as all this bare rock indicates (foreground).

Lower Bald Eagle Creek stays full and productive in summer because Spring Creek, a large limestone with consistent flow, empties into it.

below one of the largest of these springs. I first checked the temperature in the main river just below the limestone spring and was amazed at the 66-degree reading. I then checked the temperature of the river just above the spring. Here I recorded a reading of 73 degrees Fahrenheit.

Bob and Jim began casting in that cooler water below the spring and in the next two hours landed ten Juniata holdover brown trout. None of those fish would have been found above the creek inlet.

That's what cool water will do for you in the heat of the summer. If you know the Frankstown Branch of the Juniata River, you know that it flows for miles below Roaring Springs without holding many trout. But after Piney and Clover Creeks and a half dozen other small limestone streams and springs enter the main stem, wild brown trout become plentiful.

But that's not the only advantage limestone streams have. The same insect hatches that appear on freestone and limestone streams often appear in heavier numbers and a larger size on the latter. Compare the size of the Green Drake on limestone water like Penns Creek and the same insect on a freestone stream like Pine Creek in north-central Pennsylvania. On Penns

Creek you have to match the natural with a size-6 or size-8 extended-bodied fly. On Pine Creek you can get away with a size-10 pattern to match the same hatch.

Or compare the Green Drakes on Yellow Creek with those on small fertile freestone streams like Cedar Run and Slate Run. The same species averages a good hook size or two smaller on these freestone streams than it does on Yellow Creek.

Also check out the number of mayflies on a freestone versus a limestone stream. For every drake you see on a freestone you might see ten to twenty on a highly fertile, unpolluted limestone stream.

The difference between a freestone and limestone streams becomes even more evident if you fish the same hatch on the two waters late in the season. Try fishing the Trico on a limestone stream one day and then on a freestone stream the next day. On the limestone stream you'll probably see plenty of trout feeding on the spent Trico spinners in cool water. On the other hand, fish the Trico on a freestone like the Loyalsock north of Williamsport, Pennsylvania, and you'll encounter low water and temperatures over the 70-degree mark. Many freestone streams hold good Trico hatches but few hold the flow and stream temperatures needed to complete the cycle for a great matching-the-hatch day.

Lastly, limestone waters often harbor brilliantly colored wild brown trout, fish with greater coloration than you'll see on freestone streams. Take a look at the coloration of a wild Spruce Creek brown trout and you'll be in awe at what these limestone streams produce.

WHERE ARE LIMESTONE STREAMS FOUND?

If you read some of the articles and books on limestone streams you probably hold the idea that they occur mainly in southern Pennsylvania. But, limestone streams—and good ones—can also be found in Maryland, Virginia, and West Virginia. (There are also good limestones out West, and in the Midwest where they're called "spring creeks," such as in Missouri.) All of these boast some great limestone waters with some spectacular hatches. We'll examine some of these waters in chapters 2 and 3.

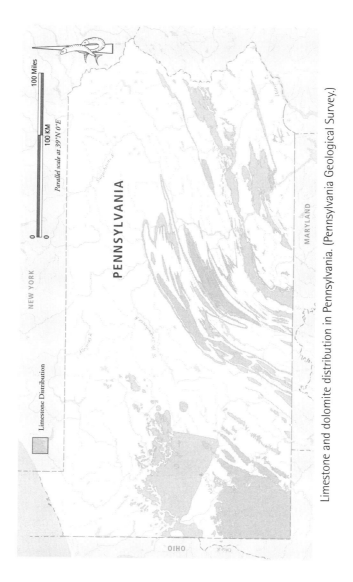

Limestone and dolomite distribution in Pennsylvania. (Pennsylvania Geological Survey.)

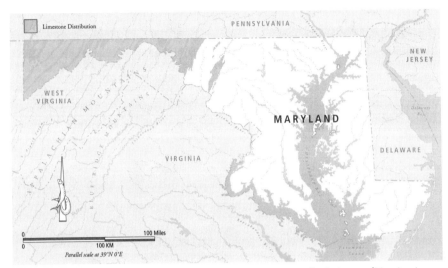

Generalized geologic map of Maryland. Limestone stream areas in dark gray. (Maryland Geological Survey.)

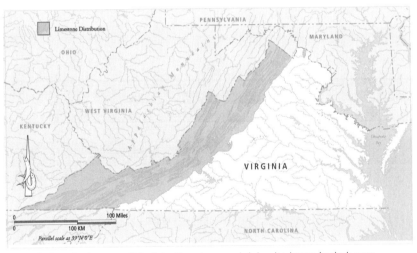

Simplified geologic map of Virginia. Limestone and dolomite layers in dark gray. (Geology Department, College of William and Mary.)

2

The Essential Limestone Streams of Pennsylvania

Where do you find limestone streams? Wherever you have water flowing through limestone and dolomite bedrock. The maps in chapter 1 show you where some of these streams are found in Maryland, Pennsylvania, and Virginia; central, south-central, and southeastern Pennsylvania have especially been blessed with these waters, and we'll focus on them first. In the following pages you'll find a brief discussion about each water.

I have rated each stream from four to ten; ten being the highest score. To arrive at each rating I considered the number and density of the hatches, the number and size of trout, and whether the stream has a good supply of stream-bred trout. I also give a general overview of the stream in a few words. Many of the limestone streams have special regulations. If the water holds a specially regulated area I list that. If you see two separate regulations, that means that the stream holds more than one regulated area. (Stream designations change from year to year—check your latest fish commission rules and regulations to be certain. That same booklet will tell you where the regulated water is located.) Each stream discussion here contains DeLorme state map directions. For example, with the Little Juniata River, "page 61, D-6 and D-7," means that the stream is listed in the Pennsylvania DeLorme map on page 61 in sections D-6 and D-7.

Kurt Thomas with a very nice rainbow trout taken on a private section of Spruce Creek. The lunker fell for a Sulphur Nymph.

CENTRAL PENNSYLVANIA

Streams: Buffalo Run—Half Moon Run—Logan Branch—Lower Bald Eagle Creek—Spring Creek—Spruce Creek—Warriors Mark Run

Rivers: Juniata River—Little Juniata River—Frankstown Branch (Little Juniata River)

Central Pennsylvania, an area from State College to the east for thirty or forty miles and to the southwest about forty to fifty miles, holds some of the more famous trout streams of the East. Within ten miles of State College you can fish Spring Creek, lower Bald Eagle Creek, Logan Branch, and a number of other productive limestone waters. Most of these streams harbor a great population of trout and some notable and fishable hatches. We will look at some of these great hatches in chapter 4.

Buffalo Run
Rating: 4
Spring Creek tributary; headwater pollution with Interstate 99 construction.
DeLorme page 62, B-1, A-2

I first looked at this small limestone stream that closely parallels State Route (SR) 550 back in 1958; I was watching two bass-fishing friends sein for minnows at Fillmore. When they showed me a net full of small brown trout, I got excited. That June I fly fished just upstream from Bellefonte. Buffalo Run hosted a heavy Sulphur hatch that continued throughout the entire afternoon that day.

But that was almost fifty years ago and much has changed. Buffalo Run runs with much less volume now. Hundreds of new homes in the Buffalo Valley have lowered the water table. (You'll read about the problem of urbanization in chapter 7.) Also, the work on Interstate 99 through the Bald Eagle and Nittany Valleys uncovered and exposed thousands of tons of iron pyrite. When exposed and combined with water this rock creates sulfuric acid. If not neutralized this acid will bring the end of any trout fishing on Buffalo Run.

Meantime the stream still boasts a good number of brown trout and a few good hatches. Yet how much longer will this small limestone stream continue to hold a good supply of wild brown trout? State Route 550 parallels this 10- to 15-foot-wide stream from Fillmore to Bellefonte.

Half Moon Creek
Rating: 5
Tributary to Spruce; small, seldom fished; all wild fish.
DeLorme page 61, B-7 and C-7

This small stream flows through western Centre County. My son, Bryan, had one of his most memorial days as a boy on Half Moon Creek, catching twelve brown trout in one afternoon. The 10-foot-wide, six-mile-long stream begins near SR 550 at Centennial and enters Spruce Creek at the town of Pennsylvania Furnace. The stream holds few hatches, but the Little Blue-Winged Olive is common.

Logan Branch
Rating: 7
Productive water in a not-so-pretty location.
DeLorme page 62, B-2

What a shame this tremendous limestone stream doesn't flow through a more pristine environment. When you fish this fertile water you are never more than fifty feet from busy SR 144, so there is little or no atmosphere here. If you don't hear cars then you are fishing in somebody's backyard. Despite all of the negatives, Logan Branch holds some behemoth brown trout and some fairly respectable hatches. Throughout the summer you will see a few Tricos and some Blue Quills. But one of the heaviest hatches and one that trout seek out most often is the Sulphur first appearing in mid-May. The most unusual hatch on this cold water is the Big Slate Drake that appears in mid-August. If you arrive on the stream around 7 P.M. you'll see some of these huge mayfly spinners high in the air above the water. Logan Branch runs cold in its entire five-mile trip from Pleasant Gap to Bellefonte where it flows into Spring Creek.

Were it not for the unsightly borders on this 20-foot-wide stream and the fish commission hatcheries at its upper end, Logan Branch would be one of my favorite limestone waters in the East. As it is now, this is shameful waste of a potentially top stream. But if it were any different then the stream would probably be totally private and heavily fished.

Why hasn't Logan become private fishing water? Unlike Elk Creek and Spruce Creek, the land bordering Logan Branch isn't held in big parcels. Where one land owner controls almost six miles of Spruce Creek, most homeowners and landowners along Logan Branch own a couple hundred feet each at most.

If you don't mind fishing in a suburban environment, this sleeper water can offer some good catches.

Lower Bald Eagle Creek (North)
Rating: 8
Large stream with plenty of deep water.
DeLorme page 62, A-2, A-3

Upstream from Milesburg Bald Eagle Creek runs warm and low with a preponderance of smallmouth bass in midsummer. Below Milesburg the same stream remains cools and flows almost bank full through much of the summer and holds plenty of trout. Why this pleasing change? One reason: Spring Creek enters Bald Eagle Creek in Milesburg. Upstream from Milesburg, Bald Eagle exhibits every character of a freestone stream. After Spring Creek enters it, Bald Eagle shows evidence of all the characteristics of a limestone stream. You'll find some fantastic large-stream fishing from Milesburg downstream five miles to Sayres Lake.

The lower Bald Eagle has quickly become one of my favorite waters in the East for numerous reasons. The state plants plenty of fingerlings in the water and they develop rapidly, and I have never seen the water temperature on this wide stream rise much above 70 degrees in the heat of the summer. There are many sections where access is fairly limited and reached only by walking a few hundred yards, and they include some prolific deep pools and productive riffles. The lower Bald Eagle doesn't experience the heavy fishing pressure so common on many of the limestone streams and holds some respectable hatches where you can fish over rising trout. Don't overlook the Green Caddis hatch that appears in early May. On May 5 several years ago I caught a number of carp (yes, carp) on dry flies during the Green Caddis hatch. A larger down-wing version emerges on July mornings.

Lower Bald Eagle Creek experiences little angling pressure, so you've got room to work the good riffles and productive pools.

Probably the top hatch of the year on the lower Bald Eagle is the Sulphur. I still remember an incident that occurred more than a decade ago just above the Curtin Bridge. I hit a hatch of afternoon Sulphurs and had several heavy trout feeding in front of me. I hooked what I thought was a heavy fish and it broke off almost immediately. I hurriedly tied on another Sulphur pattern and began casting to another riser in the same general vicinity where I lost the last fish. On the first cast I hooked the riser and netted it five minutes later—a nice 18-incher. On the right side of its mouth was my fly attached to my leader. On the left side of its mouth I saw a second fly, the very one I had just lost a minute before. How do I know? It was a Vernille-Bodied Sulphur and I think I'm the only one who ties the pattern that way.

You can match hatches all summer long on this water. As I said earlier, in July and August you'll see some Green Caddis emerging just about every morning and a fairly consistent Trico hatch and spinner fall. Even a few White Flies appear in late August near the Curtin Bridge.

In my thirty years of fishing this 60- to 100-foot-wide stream I have landed at least a half dozen trout over 20 inches long. The lower Bald Eagle holds plenty of deep pools and undercut banks that hide an abundance of lunker trout. Between these deep pools you'll find plenty of long, deep, flat runs.

I especially like the section underneath the I-80 bridge. I often wonder when I fish below this interstate bridge how many people as they travel on that highway realize that they are crossing one of the finest streams in the East. The stream holds trout and cool water from the Milesburg Bridge downstream to Sayre Lake. State Route 150 parallels the stream to the north and SR 1006 to the south. Access to the stream is easier from the south. Respect the landowners on this gem—walk in and carry your trash out.

Spring Creek

Rating: 8

Heritage Angling water. Heavily fished throughout the year.

DeLorme page 62, B-1, B-2

I still remember vividly the first time I ever drove along Spring Creek in 1956. On that late May evening I had to stop several times to clean the windshield. Coffin Flies (the Green Drake spinner) mistook the black pavement closely paralleling the creek for a stream as they moved up and down the road in their mating flight. That was the first and the last time I ever experienced that hatch on that limestone stream. Just a year or two later a slug of pollution destroyed the Green Drake and many other hatches for generations to come. The Green Drake has never reappeared.

Yes, just like the Little Juniata River, Spring Creek has valiantly withstood the advances of civilization, but with some noticeable damage to its character. In the last fifty years it has experienced some sewage problems, and then later some chemical spills. As a result of the two major debacles many hatches once prevalent on this top-notch stream are now gone. Spring Creek at one time held a respectable Brown Drake hatch. That's now gone. The tremendous Green Drake hatch and spinner fall is wiped out, probably forever. If you ever take a trip to the Pennsylvania State University Campus you must visit the Frost Museum. In that facility you'll see some of the specimens of hatches that once appeared on Spring Creek. Many have since vanished because of the advance of civilization.

Despite constant battles with pollution and urbanization, Spring Creek remains a premier limestone stream in the East. Thanks to property owned by the Pennsylvania Fish and Boat Commission much of this famous limestone stream will remain in public hands and open to fishing forever.

The stream begins near Linden Hall with one of its feeder limestone streams, Cedar Run. Other tributaries include Thompson Run which begins at the Duck Pond in State College and Slab Cabin Run which begins as a freestone stream near Pine Grove Mills. Both have some limestone influence. Parts of Slab Cabin Run just upstream from South Atherton Street in State College often dry up in the middle of the summer. The stream flows through Lemont, past some Fish Commission hatcheries, and through the town of Bellefonte where it picks up additional cool flow from Logan Branch and Buffalo Run. Spring Creek holds plenty of trout and much of it remains open to public fishing from Lemont to Milesburg where it joins the Bald Eagle Creek.

Hatches continue to be fairly sparse after bouts with pollution. Prominent ones that remain are the Little Blue-Winged Olive Dun, Trico, and Sulphur. The Sulphur hatch is one of the heaviest I've encountered. The Sulphur hatch brings out hordes of anglers and creates extremely crowded conditions. You can fish midge hatches most of the winter at Fisherman's Paradise, a section of the stream owned by the Fish Commission.

Expect to see angling pressure almost any month you visit this famous limestone. Spend some time on the Pennsylvania Fish and Boat Commission water that begins near a section locals call the Rock. It's where Rock Road and Houserville Road intersect. There is about three miles of top-notch fishing until you see Shiloh Road. You can also access the stream at Shiloh Road or at Fisherman's Paradise just a couple miles downstream.

Spring Creek might be Pennsylvania's best-known limestone stream, and thus sees steady angling pressure well into December.

You'll find some of the best matching-the-hatch opportunities and fewer anglers on the lower section of Spring Creek, from Bellefonte to Milesburg. Here you'll encounter bigger water and some stretches relatively less easy to access. I especially like the area around the Bellefonte sewage plant on the lower end.

Spruce Creek

Rating: 8

Catch-and-release water; mostly private and fee fishing.

DeLorme page 61, C-7

Most of Spruce Creek has been private for many, many years. The only major section, about a half-mile long, is the Penn State University area two miles upstream from its mouth. Since it is the only major area open to public fishing, this section gets pounded throughout the year.

Even though much of the water is private you can still fish some of it for a fee. The last half mile of the stream, before it enters the Little Juniata River at the town of Spruce Creek, is loosely run as a fee-fishing area. Above that Donny Beaver (877-788-9797) owns a quarter mile and leases out other parcels for fishing. Above Donny Beaver's operation there is a section called the Colerain Club. A couple miles above the Colerain Club, Wayne Harpster (814-632-5925) owns a good deal of the stream. For a reasonable fee he allows anglers to fish and stay overnight at two cabins on his property. Each cabin has approximately a mile of fertile limestone water with plenty of big trout. Annually, in late May, Jimmy Carter usually stays and fishes at one of his cabins. Many call Wayne the Baron of Spruce Creek since he owns more than seven miles of this top limestone stream. In addition there are two fly shops on Spruce Creek and both guide anglers for a fee. Spruce Creek Fly Shop (814-632-0073) operated by Skip and Sandy Galbraith and Eric Stroup opened in May 2004. They guide on a picturesque upper section of Spruce located near Graysville. Al Bright (814-632-3071) operates Spruce

Dave McMullen releases a nice brown trout on the Donny Beaver section of Spruce Creek.

Creek Outfitters and employs guides who take clients on the Colerain section of the stream.

Spruce Creek begins with a spring near the small town of Rockspring. Two miles downstream, just above the town of Pennsylvania Furnace, dozens of additional limestone springs enter the main stem. State Route 45 parallels the creek on its fifteen-mile-plus journey to the Little Juniata River.

The Green Drake hatch appears on the lower half of the stream in the last week of May. At the same time you can see the Sulphur, Slate Drake, and Blue-Winged Olive Dun. The Sulphur is one of the heaviest hatches on the stream. Spruce Creek also boasts a great Olive Sulphur hatch (*Ephemerella needhami*). Even in mid-April, anglers are greeted by the famous down-wing hatch, the Grannom. This caddis fly continues appearing daily until late April.

The stream has some pollution concerns, mainly manure spills. At least three times excessive organic matter has accidentally spilled into the stream. One of these events killed a good number of trout. The late, famous outdoor writer Jim Bashline, who lived along the stream, told me he saw huge brown trout actually jump out of the stream and onto the bank when the one pollution event occurred.

Even though most of this famous limestone is private it's well worth the trip to pay to fish.

Warriors Mark Run
Rating: 6
Tributary to Spruce; mostly private water, but some good hatches.
DeLorme page 61, C-6

How many times have I crossed over this stream at Huntingdon Furnace and noted spinners in the air on Warriors Mark Run? Would you believe hundreds of times? I have seen Sulphur spinners, Trico spinners, and even some Coffin Flies just downstream. Twenty-foot-wide Warriors Mark Run begins near the town of the same name. It flows for about six miles before it enters Spruce Creek. It is a highly productive limestone but mainly private. In fact, a private club from nearby Tyrone controls more than a mile of the water in the Huntingdon Furnace area. Below there, from Camp Kanasatake downstream, Warriors Mark Run holds a respectable Green Drake hatch.

LARGE CENTRAL PENNSYLVANIA RIVERS AFFECTED BY LIMESTONE FEEDER STREAMS

Some larger rivers in central Pennsylvania receive beneficial discharges from limestone springs which in turn help them support surprising numbers of trout. Normally you think of these bigger rivers as homes for bass, catfish, and other common warm water species. But add a discharge of cool water from a limestone spring and all things change. The Little Juniata River wouldn't be nearly the river it is now if it didn't get the cool limestone water I talked about earlier. In its journey from Bellwood to the town

Warriors Mark Run, cows and all, exemplifies the farmland limestone, but much of its mileage is private.

of Spruce Creek at least nine limestone springs and streams enter the main stem. These range in size from Spruce Creek to several tiny limestone springs that appear above the surface just a few yards before they enter the river. The Little Juniata River, the Frankstown Branch, and the main stem of the Juniata River hold trout in some areas because of the influx of limestone springs. The same goes for the lower Bald Eagle Creek. We'll look at these waters even though they are not true limestone streams, but because they are all affected by limestone water entering them.

The Juniata River
Rating: 5
Fish the river below Petersburg where springs enter.
DeLorme page 61, D-7

Below the confluence of the Little Juniata and the Frankstown Branch, I have caught brown trout over 20 inches long in the main stem of the Juniata where cool limestone springs enter just above and below the hamlet of Warrior Ridge. Even in July and August, if you know where these springs are, you can catch trout. The water above these springs might be 75 to 80 degrees, but the trout stay within range of the cooler waters.

How do you find out where these limestone springs enter larger rivers? I spent many cold days in January and February searching them out. I look for openings in the ice. Many freestone rivers almost completely clog up in midwinter with surface ice, but rivers and streams remain relatively ice-free where limestone springs enter. It only makes sense: In the winter the waters entering from limestone springs are warmer than the freestone waters and therefore freeze less often or not at all.

The time to fish this section of the Juniata River is when the Sulphur appears. For this is the time—mid-May to mid-June—that huge browns feed on the surface. Look also for the White Fly in late August as brown trout rise to that hatch.

Most limestone springs enter the main stem from the east side of the river from Petersburg downriver to Huntingdon. Just below Petersburg the river is dammed. Even in that section you'll find one or two limestone springs entering from the east. Most of the limestone streams that do enter the main stem of the river erupt above the surface a hundred feet or so before they enter the river.

The Little Juniata River
Rating: 9
All-tackle trophy trout section; one of the best year-round fisheries in the East.
DeLorme page 61, C-6, D-7

The Little Juniata River has had its highs and lows in the past fifty years. Before 1970 this river carried all kinds of pollutants on its trip to the main stem near Petersburg. Raw sewage poured into the LJ from upstream communities, and tannic colored water from paper mills polluted and discolored the water. Few anglers fished the river at that time and even fewer cared what happened to it. Even then—when it carried all of these pollutants—the river held plenty of behemoth brown trout and hosted some fine hatches. But the best was yet to come. In the early 1970s efforts to clean the river succeeded and the LJ boasted more hatches and plenty of brown trout. It flowed clean and free of most odiferous pollutants. The peak history of this river and its brown trout population ran from 1972 to 1996. It was this era when the river boasted its best hatches and biggest fighting trout. Along with that came hordes of anglers to fish the famous hatches.

Since 1996 the river has regressed a bit, having received several additional doses of contaminants from the railroad and other lesser-known chemical spills. During a flooding episode in January 1996 additional contaminants leaked into the river from what many believe were barrels of buried pesticides. For several years after that event the trout in the river looked emaciated. No wonder: these trout had incredibly little in the way of aquatic food on which to feed as the river was almost void of mayfly hatches—no more Green Drakes, few Sulphurs, and no White Flies.

The LJ has since begun to recover and attain its rightful place as one of the top streams in the East. It will take time. The Sulphur and White Fly have reappeared in more limited numbers, and in late May 2004 enough Green Drakes appeared to make a fishable hatch. The hatch should grow heavier in the next few years. Look for the Green Drake on the river in the last days of May.

Twenty years ago the LJ held a fantastic Green Caddis in early May. That hatch has waned and the Grannom has now become the important down-wing hatch. This latter caddisfly appears on the water in mid- to late April and brings trout to the surface for two weeks.

Over its brief history as a top trout river in the United States, the Little Juniata has acquired something else: friends. When it ran discolored and polluted thirty years ago no one cared about it. After anglers began fishing these fertile waters, hitting some of the spectacular hatches and catching hefty brown trout they become advocates of this fine river. If you are interested in helping this river contact Eric Stroup (814-632-0073).

What happens when a river comes to prominence? Often private club waters develop. At the present time a battle rages between some environmental organizations, state agencies, and a local landowner on the Little Juniata. The state and the organizations argue that the river is considered a navigable one and therefore the local landowner cannot bar anglers from fishing the water. The courts should decide sometime in 2005 on this important, far-ranging decision.

The LJ holds trout from above Bellwood downriver to Petersburg. The state has just designated a section near Bellwood as a Delayed Harvest water. Special trophy trout regulations apply below Tyrone.

I said earlier that at least nine limestone streams and springs enter the river's main stem in its twenty-five-mile journey, adding plenty of nutrients and cold water to the river. Two of these streams hold trout and hatches. Logan Spring and Elk Run enter the main stem from opposite sides just downriver from Tyrone. Logan holds a Trico hatch and Elk holds some large brown trout.

The Frankstown Branch of the Juniata River

Rating: 7

Fish the riffles from Williamsburg to Water Street.

DeLorme page 61, D-6; page 75, A-6

The Frankstown Branch of the Juniata River holds a good population of stream-bred brown trout. It has become a vital fishery because it receives inflows from at least five small- to medium-sized limestone feeders on its trip from Williamsburg downriver to Water Street. Above the town of Williamsburg the Frankstown Branch is a poor, warm freestone stream (with some limestone influence from Beaverdam Creek) suffering from various impurities. In its upper reaches around Claysburg the state plants trout. Just above Williamsburg, where Piney Creek enters, the river runs cooler, and you can pick up some trophy trout all summer long, especially in the faster water. A couple miles below Piney Creek another fairly large limestone stream, Clover Creek, enters the Frankstown Branch. At least four more named limestone streams and many unnamed springs and runs enter the main stem from Mt. Etna downriver to Water Street. Yellow Spring Run, Roaring Run and Fox Run enter near Mt. Etna. Canoe Valley Run enters at Water Street. This last stream boasts a good number of brown trout. All of these add cool water to this large river.

Any sizable riffle in the Frankstown Branch from Williamsburg downriver to Water Street holds a good number of trout. All of them are hefty, wild brown trout. The hatch of the season on this 100-foot-wide river is the Sulphur. When these mayflies appear you'll see plenty of 15-inch-plus brown trout feeding on the surface. The hatch begins around mid-May and continues though early June. Look for the hatch in the riffled water just at dusk.

The section from Water Street upriver to Mt. Etna can be reached only by foot on the Rails-to-Trails lower trail that parallels the river for almost fifteen miles. Recently Rails-to-Trails has set up parking lots from Water Street to Williamsburg giving anglers even more access to the river. Were it not for this great organization this water and others in the state would not

A typical stretch of the Frankstown Branch of the Juniata River. Fish above Williamsburg to find the bigger trout.

be nearly as accessible. Thanks are due to people like Larry Williamson, Director of the Department of Conservation and Natural Resources' Bureau of Recreation and Conservation—and a fly fisher in his own right—and Palmer Brown of Rails-to-Trails of Central Pennsylvania. Palmer was the organizing force behind the Lower Trail. Support Rails-to-Trails as much as possible.

The lowest point on the river where I have consistently caught trout is at Water Street. I have even fished over trout rising to White Flies in mid-August in that area. I mentioned before that here the prolific and productive Canoe Valley Run enters, giving an added slug of cold limestone water to the river.

I said earlier that the areas where I consistently catch trout on the river are the riffled sections. There is a total of about twelve miles of trout water. When the temperature rises, fish the faster riffled water. Respect these wild trout and remember this section is not stocked and is totally dependent on anglers returning their trout. Please don't kill any trout here.

Paul Weamer takes a nice stream-bred brown during an early Sulphur hatch on the Frankstown Branch.

CENTRAL PENNSYLVANIA—EASTERN REGION

Antes Creek—Big Fishing Creek—Cedar Run—Elk Creek—Lick Run—
Little Fishing Creek—Long Run—Penns Creek—Pine Creek

Here's where you'll find the some of the greatest streams in the East. Penns Creek and Fishing Creek are two of the finest limestone streams in the country. And here is also where you'll find the Green Drake in its heaviest numbers.

Antes Creek
Rating: 6
Mostly private fishing.
DeLorme page 49, C-7

As a limestone stream, Antes Creek seems out of place. It's one of the northernmost limestone streams in Pennsylvania. Antes Creek begins near the small town of Oriole in southwestern part of Lycoming County. Antes flows north for five miles before it empties into the West Branch of the Susquehanna River near the town of Jersey Shore. Much of Antes is private water. Some of the lower section is run as a private club called the Antes Creek Club.

Antes Creek holds some heavy brown trout, but it has seen some pollution in the past. In 1972 when Hurricane Agnes hit the Northeast it created a flood on Antes Creek. The high water washed a slug of limestone effluent from an upstream mining operation and it coated part of the stream bed. You can still see the effects on the stream bed more than thirty years later.

But this 30-foot-wide stream is still worth a trip. If you get an opportunity to fish it, take the time. You will see Sulphurs and some Blue Quills on the water. State Route 44 parallels much of the five miles of limestone water.

Big Fishing Creek
Rating: 9
Trophy-trout section; catch-and-release regulations; great hatches in the Narrows.
DeLorme page 63, A-4 and A-5; page 49, D-4 and D-5

Most limestone streams meander slowly though farmland on their flow downstream. Not so with Big Fishing Creek. When you think of atypical limestone streams, Big Fishing Creek has got to be one of them.

It begins on farmland near Loganton in central Pennsylvania and flows intermittently for the next couple miles. Once the stream flows past the hatchery it takes on a completely different face. It is no longer the typical slow meandering farmland limestone stream, but moves rapidly through a heavily wooded deep valley or gorge that locals call the "Narrows." This four-mile-long area holds plenty of wild brook trout and stream-bred brown trout, some fantastic hatches, and plenty of cool, somewhat off-color water. Once the stream flows past a second hatchery four miles downstream at Lamar it again assumes the more typical nature of a limestone stream, flowing more slowly through farmland. A one-mile-long section that passes under I-80 often dries up in midsummer.

Hatches in the two distinct types of water on Fishing Creek are quite different. In the lower end you'll find at least two great Blue-Winged Olive

The Narrows section of Big Fishing Creek holds wild brookies and stream-bred brown trout.

hatches and a consistent Trico through August and September. Upstream the Narrows section harbors good Green Drake and Sulphur hatches and plenty of early spring mayflies like the Hendrickson, Quill Gordon, and the Blue Quill. At any given time in April you will likely witness four different mayflies, one caddisfly, and one stonefly appearing at the same time. I have experienced many days where I have fished over trout rising to hatches in April from 11 A.M. to 4 P.M. Big Fishing Creek in the Narrows section is a miniature Henry's Fork because of the number and intensity of the hatches it holds.

Big Fishing Creek holds trout and hatches its entire length until it empties into Bald Eagle Creek near Lock Haven. Pressure on the water is heaviest in the specially regulated Narrows area. Here you'll find anglers fishing throughout the season. Much of this section is closed to Sunday fishing. Below the stream flows through farmland and gets little fishing pressure until it empties into Bald Eagle at Lock Haven.

Hatches are heavy and prolific and begin early on the water. I said earlier that you'll see at least five hatches from mid-April to early May. In late May the March Brown and Slate Drake appear. Because of the cool water the Green Drake doesn't normally appear on the Narrows stretch until early to mid-June. The lower section holds more consistent hatches after late June than does the Narrows, so move downstream to fish over trout rising to summer Blue Quills, Tricos, and Blue-Winged Olives.

Cedar Run
Rating: 5
Private land, not stocked; only a few public areas.
DeLorme page 49, D-4

Cedar Run begins at the Cedar Spring Trout Hatchery. At Parvin it picks up additional flow before it enters Big Fishing Creek at Cedar Spring. This creek holds a great Sulphur hatch in mid-May. Travel up and down the road paralleling the stream, Local Route 2018, at dusk in mid-May and you'll see plenty of Sulphur spinners. There are Tricos, too. This is not a stocked stream, though it holds a number of decent brown trout, and much of it is private. Owners Jim and Joe Tomalonis of the trout hatchery say that there are only a few sections open to fishing. Permission for access is required.

Elk Creek
Rating: 7
Much of the upper half is private water.
DeLorme page 63, A-5 and B-5

Some of the greatest hatches I have ever witnessed occurred on this 30- to 40-foot-wide stream just about thirty miles east of State College. I often fished Elk Creek on the opening day of the trout season in Pennsylvania. The state stopped stocking this stream in the mid 1980s, but they over-looked one cardinal rule when they did that: They neglected to procure access to much of the stream. What happened? Much of the stream that I fished just fifteen years ago has now been posted against trespassing. All those hatches, all those trout—yet now we are forever banned from fishing there. There are small sections of the upper end still open to public fishing, but the privatization has begun and it probably won't take too long until it becomes totally private. What a shame some state organizations have not been more proactive.

I get more upset about private water on this stream than any other be-cause this is the limestone stream I call home. This is the limestone stream where I conducted much of my insect research. I sat, watched, and studied the hatches on this stream when I prepared my manuscript for *Meeting and Fishing the Hatches*. This is where I fished almost daily throughout the season.

Elk Creek holds some great hatches that begin with the Blue Quill and Little Blue-Winged Olive Dun in April to the Trico and Blue Quill that compete for air space in the fall. It even boasts a respectable March Brown and Dark Green Drake in late May. But, again, the heaviest hatch on Elk Creek is the Sulphur. More than ten years ago my son, Bryan, Vince

Gigliotti, and I hit a Sulphur hatch that began in a fine drizzle at 10 A.M. and continued through much of the afternoon. We caught well over fifty trout during that hatch.

Were it not for Elk Creek and its major tributary, Pine Creek, Penns Creek would not be nearly the trout stream it is. Elk begins near Smullton and flows southwest to Spring Bank then south through Millheim to Coburn where it joins Penns Creek. Smullton and Elk Creek roads parallel much of the upper one-fifth of the stream. The Narrows Road gets you to Elk Creek just above Millheim then SR 2011 to the creek mouth at Coburn.

Lick Run
Rating: 5
Trophy-trout section; a very small stream.
DeLorme page 62, A-4; page 48, D-3

This four-mile-long narrow limestone stream begins near Jacksonville along SR 26 in eastern Centre County before it enters Foster Joseph Sayers Lake. The upper end flows through fields and the lower end through woodlands. Lick Run ranges from 10 to 15 feet wide but it does harbor some fairly large brown trout.

If you enjoy fishing small streams and possess casting finesse to cope with high weeds, bushes, and trees, then you might enjoy Lick Run. As you travel along SR 26 just south of Howard you'll see at least two springs entering to form Lick Run. The inlets of these streams might be worth a try.

Little Fishing Creek
Rating: 5
Freestone in headwaters with some nice brook trout.
DeLorme page 62–63, 4-A and 5-A; page 49, D-4

Little Fishing Creek flows for about twelve miles before it enters Big Fishing Creek in the town of Lamar. This limestone stream begins in Greens

Valley just east of Pleasant Gap and flows northeast. The first five or six miles of this Little Fishing Creek is a classic small, 10- to 20-foot-wide free-stone steam filled with native brook trout. You can access this upper area off a dead-end forest road, Greens Valley Road. This freestone stream then flows north through Mingoville. From Mingoville downstream to its con-fluence with Big Fishing Creek the stream is limestone in nature. From Mingoville to Lamar the 20-foot-wide stream holds some fairly deep pools. This lower end parallels SR 64. I have never seen spectacular hatches on this lower water, but it has some interesting pools and riffles.

Long Run
Rating: 6
Great mountain stream.
DeLorme page 49, D-5

If you like fly fishing pocket water, riffles, and deep pools, you'll enjoy fish-ing Long Run near Lock Haven. In its headwaters near I-80, this 10-foot-wide freestone stream, formed by the junction of Spruce and Pepper Runs, holds plenty of brook trout. Then, in the middle section of its eight-mile journey to Big Fishing Creek at Salona, Long Run widens to 15 or 20 feet and seems to have some limestone influence. It looks like a miniature Big Fishing Creek above Lamar (the locals, again, call this stretch the "Nar-rows") and the state plants trout here.

Near the town of Rote, Long Run flows underground and doesn't ap-pear on the surface (except for spring runoff and heavy rains) until it reaches Salona. When it does appear the last mile or two of its journey it is truly limestone in nature.

Hatches on the upper end include the Quill Gordon, Blue Quill, and Hendrickson. There are some Tricos and Sulphurs on the limestone end of this unusual stream. Hatches vary considerably from the top to the bottom of Long Run.

State Route 477 closely parallels much of Long Run. To reach the stream to fish you often have to climb down a steep 30- to 40-foot bank.

Penns Creek

Rating: 10—the best in the East.

All-tackle trophy trout section; catch-and-release regulations.

DeLorme page 63, B-5, 6, and 7

I wrote in *Trout Streams and Hatches of Pennsylvania* about a Fourth of July in 1979 on Penns Creek, the famous but sometimes frustrating limestone stream in central Pennsylvania. I said in that book that by 10 A.M. the temperature had barely reached 58 degrees, and a fine drizzle fell. At the lower end of the catch-and-release section two fair-weather anglers returned to their cars, seemingly disgusted with the depressing weather. As the only nut remaining on the entire stretch, I headed up the abandoned railroad bed toward the R. B. Winter estate where thousands of Blue-Winged Olive Duns floated, half-dazed, swirling around in an eddy. Normally this species (*Drunella cornutella*) takes off rapidly from the surface when emerging, but the unusually cold weather today prevented the duns from escaping quickly from the water. Five, ten, fifteen trout rose in a small riffle in front of me. In three hours I caught sixty-five fish.

After the first edition of *Trout Streams* appeared I received a letter from Andrew Leitzinger of Collegeville, Pennsylvania. Apparently I wasn't alone on Penns that day, twenty-six years ago. Andrew fished the hatch two miles upstream from me. He wrote:

> On July 4, 1979, in the late morning after a cold rain, I fished the upper no-kill stretch of Penns Creek from the Broadwaters to the Upper Island. I found the surface covered with Blue-Winged Olive mayflies. I fished this stretch and hooked and released thirty trout between 10 and 17 inches long. I missed many, many more. The water surface was quite broken as far as you could see with feeding fish.
>
> I fished that day in complete solitude (I thought). I was cold, happy, and alone. I can remember how my shoulders ached from

so many hours, and my thumb had become tattered by the teeth of the many trout that I had released. I stopped fishing at about 5 P.M. because I had reached a state just short of exhaustion. I exalted the cold gray heavens above me and gave thanks for a wonderful and unique gift.

So when I read your book, *Trout Streams and Hatches of Pennsylvania*, and came across the passage on your experience at Penns Creek, I wondered what the odds were that such conditions had occurred more than once on a fourth of July in the past ten years; a cold rain, a great hatch of Blue-Winged Olives, and a nearly deserted stream. . . . But if, as I hope, those two days were one and the same, then I am glad to know that one other person was able to share the exhilaration I felt that day. Those days, when all things come together, are few and far between and should never be taken for granted.

If you listed the top fifty trout streams in the nation you would certainly have to include Penns Creek in that select group. I have experienced so many great hatches, so many matching-the-hatch episodes, that this limestone stream is one of my top choices. It consistently produces some of the greatest brown trout fishing in the East.

Many anglers associate this fertile stream with the Green Drake. Unless you enjoy fishing almost elbow-to-elbow then avoid the stream at the Green Drake time, usually from May 27 to June 5. But, it's much more than just a one-hatch stream. It holds some spectacular hatches throughout the season. The large Grannom appears in mid-April, but in recent years the numbers of this large caddisfly have significantly waned. Sulphurs often appear with Green Drakes. The larger drake often masks what the trout feed on in late May—the Sulphur. Penns holds a significant Slate Drake in late May and early June, and again in September. Long after you thought the matching-the-hatch season had ended you'll encounter Slate Drakes on Penns Creek.

Penns begins at a limestone cavern open to the public and appropriately called Penns Cave. The huge limestone spring flows immediately into

The annual rite of spring on Penns Creek is the Green Drake hatch; here anglers gather early and wait for the big flies to appear.

a lake. The section from the lake downstream to the hamlet of Spring Mills is mostly private and posted. Here you'll find a 30-foot-wide stream with plenty of stream-bred brown trout. Additional cold water enters the stream in Spring Mills, but so does Sinking Creek, a tannic, warmer stream flowing from the Bear Meadows Wilderness area.

On its flow from Spring Mills to Coburn the water runs mainly through farmland and warms considerably. Were it not for the shot of cold water from Elk Creek at Coburn, Penns Creek would not nearly be the stream it is. Elk Creek and a tributary, Pine Creek, give Penns a needed surge of cooler limestone water, creating a top eastern fishery for the next twenty miles. After Elk Creek enters, Penns expands to 100 to 150 feet wide.

I said earlier that when you ask the average fly fisher what he or she associates with Penns Creek, most people will often say the Green Drake hatch. When this hatch appears, usually around the end of May or early

June, it creates a circuslike atmosphere. You'll see the stream lined with anglers early in the evening waiting for the hatch to begin. Just finding a place to park can be a harrowing experience. But it's worth the trip to see this festival just once in a lifetime and to see the substantial mayflies fill the air near dusk.

In addition to the Green Drake, however, Penns Creek holds fantastic Sulphur and March Brown hatches. Then there is the aforementioned Blue-Winged Olive Dun hatch.

Access to the section from Coburn downstream to Cherry Run is fairly limited. You can access the area from Coburn to the old abandoned railroad tunnel at Penn View by way of a dirt road on the south side of the stream. From the tunnel to Ingleby you have to walk in on the old railroad tracks. Ingleby Road south of SR 45 takes you into the middle section. From Ingleby to Swift Run you again have to hike into the stream; Poe Paddy Road goes into the stream at Swift Run. And from Cherry Run up to Swift Run you have to walk in. Below Cherry Run there is easy access.

Because much of the riparian is farmland, Penns muddies up quickly after a rain storm and continues to run turbid for a long time after. This stream is a must to visit if you enjoy hatches, wild brown trout, and scenic getaways—just keep in mind the heavy angling pressure from mid-May through mid-June.

Pine Creek
Rating: 6
Much of the upper half is private water.
DeLorme page 63, B-5

Pine Creek is a major tributary of Elk Creek. Pine begins as a freestone stream that flows from the east in the Bald Eagle State Forest. In its first ten miles Pine Creek is a terrific, public, small freestone stream chock full of brook trout. George Harvey and I have fished this upper end frequently and have had some spectacular days with small brook trout. After the stream flows past Woodward it reemerges as a terrific 30- to 50-foot-wide limestone stream. Much of the limestone section has been recently posted, but there is an occasionally open section throughout.

The water holds plenty of Sulphurs, Blue-Winged Olive Duns, and Blue Quills. You'll even see a few Green Drakes and Tricos near where it enters Elk Creek. Pine Creek empties into Elk Creek just above the town of Coburn. Pine would even hold more hatches if it had more rocks, boulders, and debris. Pick up a submerged log on this limestone stream and you'll probably find hundreds of mayfly nymphs.

There may not be a storybook ending for this limestone stream. Pine Creek might go the way of too many of our precious streams and become totally private water. For now there are roads that access this small stream almost it entire length. As you travel north along Elk Creek turn left one mile above Coburn on SR 2018.

CENTRAL PENNSYLVANIA—WESTERN REGION
Beaverdam Creek—Canoe Creek—Clover Creek—Cove Creek—
Piney Creek—Potter Creek—Sinking Run—Yellow Creek
These are the far-west limestone streams in Pennsylvania, the waters found in Blair and Bedford Counties. Except for Yellow Creek the limestone streams in this area experience relatively light fishing pressure. Some of them even boast Green Drakes and all of them host Sulphur hatches.

Beaverdam Creek
Rating: 7
A top-notch small stream with some private water.
DeLorme page 74, B-4

I discovered this small limestone gem by sheer accident one day on my way to fish Bob's Creek in Bedford County. For several months I crossed Beaverdam Creek on my way to Bob's Creek but never gave it a second thought. That is, until I noticed an angler fishing it. I stopped and watched for a while then decided to get my fishing gear out the car. On the second cast in that small limestone I caught a twelve-inch planted trout. This small stream also holds a good number of holdover trout.

Beaverdam Creek has a decent Sulphur hatch and a fishable Trico spinner fall. The Sulphur appears as early as mid-May on the water.

Beaverdam begins just northwest of the town of Queen. It flows east, then northeast emptying into the Frankstown Branch of the Juniata River at Claysburg. This 20-foot-wide cool limestone stream has plenty of deep pools and undercut banks. You can reach the stream off I-99 at Sproul. State Route (SR) 3006 gets you to the lower end and SR 4031 to the upper end.

Canoe Creek

Rating: 6

A decent Green Drake hatch just above the lake.

DeLorme page 61, D-5

Is Canoe Creek influenced by limestone? It flows in the area of Blair County which contains limestone bedrock. It holds both a Green Drake and a fantastic Sulphur hatch. So I am convinced that Canoe Creek has some limestone character. The lower end of Canoe, below the dam, even holds some Tricos in the summer. The upper end flows through state gamelands and you have to walk to reach this section.

Clover Creek

Rating: 6

Some good Trico fishing on a stream flowing totally through farmland.

DeLorme page 75, A and B-6

Clover Creek flows six miles to the east of Piney. It empties into the Frankstown Branch just below the town of Williamsburg, adding limestone water to the main stem of the Frankstown Branch. The upper end of this stream flows through miles of farmland. In its upper reaches Clover

Creek is a 10-foot-wide limestone stream. The lower end—the last three miles—flows through mostly forested land. The stream widens considerably and before it enters the Frankstown Branch it is 30 to 40 feet wide.

Like most other limestone streams in the area, Clover holds a respectable Trico hatch in its upper end. Again, one of the heaviest hatches on this stream is the Sulphur. Look for the hatch around 8:30 P.M. from mid-May through early June. The stream begins just southwest of Henrietta. State Route 2011 parallels the upper ten miles of water.

Cove Creek
Rating: 6
A relatively undiscovered Bedford County limestone stream with some good hatches and deep pools; some private water.
DeLorme page 75, D-4; page 88, A-3 and 4

Of all the limestone streams that I've fished this has got to be near the top in those least known by the average angler. Why? It flows through an isolated valley in southwestern Pennsylvania that is difficult to find. Cove Creek begins near Beegletown and flows northeast about fifteen miles before it empties into the Raystown Branch of the Juniata River near Bedford. State Route 2017 parallels much of the stream and you can reach the upper end on SR 326. You reach the lower end off Lutzville Road (SR 2019). In its lower end, Cove Creek ranges from 30 to 50 feet wide with plenty of deep pools throughout. Its 30-foot-wide middle section flows mostly through farmland and some of it is posted. The upper end holds some deep pools with some stocked and stream-bred trout. In its upper end near Rainsburg there are some areas posted against Sunday fishing.

Cove Creek has some respectable hatches like the Green Drake, Sulphur, and Little Blue-Winged Olive Dun. If you enjoy fishing the hatches then you have got to fish Cove Creek in mid-May when the heavy Sulphur hatch appears. Bob Foor of Everett took some of the Green Drakes from this stream and successfully transplanted them more than two decades ago on Yellow Creek nearby. If you like to match the Green Drake hatch and see trout rising

Cove Creek is not as well known as other streams, but is a nice alternative to nearby Yellow Creek during the Green Drake hatch.

to this huge mayfly—and you get frustrated with the crowded conditions on Yellow Creek—Cove Creek might be for you. You reach the stream by taking Lutsville Road off U.S. Route 30 between Bedford and Everett.

Piney Creek
Rating: 7
A small limestone with little farmland.
DeLorme page 75, A and B-5

Not all limestone streams flow through fertile farmland. The upper part of Piney Creek, just ten miles east of Altoona, doesn't. This small cool stream flows for more than ten miles through woodland before it enters the Frankstown Branch of the Juniata River at Williamsburg.

Jim Heltzel and I spent many, many evenings on this pristine, productive stream when the March Brown and Sulphurs appeared. We caught our share of trout matching those two hatches, some fish up to 18 inches long. Many evenings we often left this stream well past 9:30 P.M. On many of those trips we had to stop the car several times to wipe off the splattered Sulphur spinners that thought the road was the stream.

By far the heaviest hatch Piney holds is the Sulphur. Fish it in mid- to late May and you'll see clouds of mating spinners in the air and a good supply of duns emerging on the surface around 8:30 P.M. At the same time you'll see some March Browns on the water in the afternoon.

State Route 866 parallels the upper end a mile to the south of the stream. You can reach the lower half of the stream off LR 441.

Potter Creek
Rating: 7
A good number of trout on a small limestone stream.
DeLorme page 74, C-4 and 5

For more than five years I looked forward to the Sulphur hatch on Yellow Creek. That dependable hatch in mid-May brought dozens of trout to the surface at the town of Waterside. I fished the hatch where Potter Creek entered. The hatch, the rising trout—both were completely predictable. But until a few years ago I had not fished upstream on Potter Creek. There the stream holds abundant Sulphurs, Little Blue-Winged Olives, and Tricos, yet it is relatively left alone except for some informed locals.

State Route 868 parallels much of this 20-foot-wide limestone stream. However, it is extremely difficult to find any space to park a vehicle. The stream in its lower half averages 15 to 20 feet wide. By the time you travel upstream a few miles it narrows to 10 feet wide. Potter Creek empties into Yellow Creek at the town of Waterside. If you see anyone from the Mountain Laurel Chapter of Trout Unlimited thank them for the stream improvement work they performed on the middle section of this limestone stream.

Sinking Run
Rating: 7
Private fishing, but you can fish if you stay overnight at a bed and breakfast.
DeLorme page 61, D-6

I call Sinking Run the eighth wonder of the world. Once you see it you might feel the same way. Sinking Run begins its extremely short journey with a large influx of water from an almost hidden spring. Over the eons that spring, one of the ten largest in Pennsylvania, has carved out an arch in a huge limestone formation. This arch and spring, appropriately called Arch Spring by the locals, is truly one of a kind. The spring flows above ground as Sinking Run for about a half mile before it again disappears underground. Much of the water is never seen again until it enters the Little Juniata River five miles downstream. (When rainfall is plentiful Sinking Run often flows above ground on its five-mile trip to the Little Juniata River. If rain is scarce then the stream goes underground only to emerge just as it reaches the river.)

Guess what the temperature of this stream runs in early July? Would you believe that it rarely gets above 55 degrees—even on the hottest day of the year?

I once fished this stream with Larry Csonka, the famous football player and TV-show personality, to film a segment for the show he hosted then, *Suzuki Outdoors*. I tied a Sulphur pattern streamside, and while the cameras rolled I quickly picked up two stream-bred browns. I couldn't wait for my fifteen minutes of fame when that segment was supposed to air on ESPN the following November. But the episode never ran; the cameraman ruined the video tape by getting it wet. So you'll just have to believe me— the Sulphur hatch on this small cold limestone is highly productive and lasts for several weeks. Abbreviated Sinking Run also hosts a good hatch of Dark Green Drakes. This large late-May mayfly brings trout to the surface to feed on them.

You can fish this stream if you stay at the bed and breakfast on the site owned by Dave Morrow. Dave's son, Austin Morrow, is one of the top fly fishers in the region. It is inexpensive and well worth the time to stay overnight at the bed and breakfast. The home on the property was built in the late 1700s and harbors much historical data. Don't miss a chance to fish this small stream—it is a rare opportunity. You won't necessarily catch a lot of trout, but you will enjoy fishing this extremely cool, truncated limestone stream.

Yellow Creek

Rating: 8

Delayed Harvest regulations; an increasing amount of private water.

DeLorme page 75, C-5

Even though this Bedford County limestone stream gets plenty of pressure it is one of my favorites in Pennsylvania because it holds some impressive hatches. It's a miniature Penns Creek when Green Drake enthusiasts line the bank in anticipation of the hatch, and I've seen some heavy browns taken during that hatch in the regulated water. Even though the Delayed Harvest area gets plenty of pressure it's my favorite stretch. Anglers arrive early when the drake appears. But Yellow Creek holds much more than just the Green Drake. The Sulphur appears in heavy numbers as does the March Brown.

Because it is one of the top limestone streams in the state, however, there is a fear that part of Yellow Creek might become privatized like some of the other important limestone waters. The state Fish and Boat Commission has got to be more proactive and anticipate some of these problems and actively secure rights-of-way on these valuable streams.

State Route 36 parallels the upper end of Yellow Creek. You can reach the lower end off SR 26. Anglers often prefer the regulated area because of the heavy trout population and the quality and quantity of the hatches. To reach the Delayed Harvest area turn onto SR 1024 just south of Loysburg. If you hate crowded conditions you can fish above or below the regulated area and you'll often be the only fly fisher. Some of the easiest access and

Productive stretches of Yellow Creek see good Green Drake, March Brown, and Sulphur hatches. But privatization threatens this stream.

best fly fishing is on the lower three or four miles. State Route 26 parallels much of this lower part before the stream joins the Raystown Branch of the Juniata River at Hopewell.

CENTRAL PENNSYLVANIA—SOUTHERN REGION
Honey Creek–Kishacoquillas Creek–Tea Creek
The locals who named the limestone streams around Lewistown, Pennsylvania, must have been teetotalers or Temperance Union activists. Why else would they call three local waters Honey, Tea, and Coffee? (Because lord knows how many streams might otherwise have been named Whiskey Creek or Rummy Branch.) These three and several more in the area are considered reasonably good limestone streams.

Honey Creek
Rating: 8
Some surprisingly good hatches.
DeLorme page 62 and 63, C-4

Honey Creek begins with two freestone streams, Havice Creek and Treaster Run. The two flow through forest land before they join. Shortly after they unite they disappear underground, and then reappear a couple miles downstream as a fantastic, productive limestone stream, Honey Creek.

Honey flows eight miles before it empties into the Kishacoquillas at the town of Reedsville. Honey Creek holds plenty of stream-bred trout and some great hatches. It's one of the few limestone streams that I know of that holds a respectable Brown Drake hatch. At about the same time (late May and early June) you can see Sulphurs, Green Drakes, March Browns, and Blue-Winged Olives. This 30- to 40-foot-wide limestone stream continues to be one of my favorites in the East. State Route 1002 parallels the stream its entire length.

If you like cool water, wild trout, and some great hatches then don't overlook this one. It gets little pressure; just some enthusiastic locals. Honey holds a great number of stream-bred browns and is fairly easy to access.

Honey Creek gets little pressure yet holds numerous stream-bred trout and offers a nice Brown Drake hatch.

Kishacoquillas Creek

Rating: 6

A great Sulphur hatch.

DeLorme page 62, C-3, D-3 and D-4

"Kish" Creek begins near Allensville about twenty miles to the southwest of Lewistown. It flows northeast to Reedsville where it makes an abrupt change in direction to the south. The finest fishing is from Reedsville downstream to its junction with the Juniata River in Lewistown. Here you'll find some good hatches and rising trout. The state plants plenty of trout along this stretch.

As with most limestone streams one of the best hatches on Kish is the Sulphur. The hatch commences around the end of the second week in May and continues into early June. The Sulphur is extremely reliable and once it begins you can expect to meet the dun or spinner each evening for the next few weeks.

State Route 655 parallels the Kish from Allensville to Reedsville, and SR 1005 gets you to the stream from Reedsville to Lewistown. The aesthetics are not here because a part of the lower end of the stream flows under or near the heavily traveled, limited-access U.S. 322. Regardless of the overhead traffic, the Kish holds some great hatches and plenty of trout even late in the season.

Tea Creek

Rating: 6

A small, cold trout stream.

DeLorme page 62, C-4

Tea Creek is just a small, five-mile-long, extremely cold limestone stream that flows into the Kishacoquillas at Reedsville. Much of the upper end is private, but the creek does hold trout here. You reach the upper end on SR 4001 and the lower end near Reedsville on SR 1005. There is some open water on the lower end of Tea Creek in the town of Reedsville. On this lower end you'll see some Blue Quills and Sulphurs.

SOUTH-CENTRAL PENNSYLVANIA

Big Spring Creek—Boiling Spring Run—Falling Spring Branch Creek—
Green Spring Creek—Letort Spring Run—Middle Spring—Rowe Run—
Spring Run—Yellow Breeches

Fish the limestone streams around Chambersburg, Shippensburg, and Carlisle areas and you'll get a flavor for some great fishing. Within fifty miles you can fish the likes of the Yellow Breeches, Boiling Spring, Letort Spring, Falling Spring Branch, Big Spring, Middle Spring, and Green Spring. On some of these waters Charlie Fox and Vince Marinaro conducted most of their studies and wrote many of their observations into books that fly fishers still read. Now urbanization threatens some of these great limestone streams. You can fish three or four of these in the same day: fish a Trico spinner fall on Middle Spring in the morning; then head over to Green Spring just five miles away; and then on to Big Spring in the afternoon, ten miles from Green Spring.

Big Spring Creek

Rating: 7
Heritage Angling section; some huge trout; stream needs time for a comeback.
DeLorme page 77, C-5

Just below the old hatchery on Big Spring Creek, in the area anglers refer to as the "Ditch," you'll see anglers on the pools any time of year. Here I have seen trout well over 20 inches long caught in this section, but that was a rarity. The trout here become educated quickly.

Times haven't been kind to this once great fishery. The effluent from an upstream Pennsylvania Fish and Boat Commission fish hatchery placed at the origin of this limestone stream decimated the mayflies and decreased trout propagation in the 1990s. Area anglers and other conservationists successfully closed the hatchery in 2001.

I had an opportunity to see and fish Big Spring three years after the hatchery closed. Conditions are improving, and the water is becoming much cleaner. But what took a short time to decimate will take years to recover.

Big Spring is one of the toughest trout streams in the state in which to catch trout. Sure, you see them all the time but catching them is another story. Five, six, and even seven different fly fishers pound the same water daily. Trout almost stare at you and say, "Try to catch me." I had heard some great things about a local guide, Mike Heck, of Chambersburg, and his ability to catch these trout. Mike has guided professionally for twelve years—eight as an Orvis-endorsed guide. He began fly fishing at age eight, and tied his first fly at nine. So Mike and I met in the summer of 2004 in the Ditch area at the upper end of this four-mile-long limestone water.

I still suffered from the effects of a broken arm so Mike did the casting. At the Ditch, he tied on a scud pattern he calls Mike's Shrimp (see chapter 6). It's an olive pattern, ribbed with silver wire. On the third or fourth cast Mike hooked a trout over 20 inches long. That fish swam under a log and dislodged the fly. Never mind; Mike soon had a second, and a third trout. I finally had met the match for these finicky fish—Mike Heck.

Guide Mike Heck with a beautifully colored Big Spring brook trout. The recovery of this stream is underway.

In the Ditch area, Big Spring is 20 feet wide. Downstream a mile or two, Big Spring flows 30 to 60 feet wide. There are extensive areas on this cold limestone stream that are void of trout. Where it lacks cover or depth to hide trout, planned stream improvements should greatly help.

Big Spring flows northeast into the town of Newville before it enters the Conodoguinet Creek. Big Spring Road parallels the stream from the fish hatchery to Newville.

Mike, Brad Etchberger, and I did see a few Blue Quill spinners in the air that summer day. That's a good sign. Big Spring might take a few years for its hatches to return to their formerly prominent level, but they'll come back.

If you want to experience an enjoyable day where you'll catch trout and learn many techniques in fly fishing, then contact Mike Heck (717-816-7557). In addition to Big Spring, Yellow Breeches, and the Letort, Mike guides on Spring Creek in central Pennsylvania. (See also chapter 5 to read about Mike's tactics for these tough limestone streams.)

Boiling Spring Run

Rating: 7
A very small, truncated limestone stream.
DeLorme page 77, D-6

This miniature limestone flows out of a lake created by a limestone spring and makes an abbreviated run for a few hundred yards before it empties into the Yellow Breeches Creek just below the Allenberry resort. My friend Andre Lijoi and his friend Andy Delp have landed some large trout in this 15-foot-wide fertile stream. Because the stream holds cold water and some behemoth trout it also hosts dozens of anglers daily. Access here is extremely easy even for the oldest angler. Forget fishing hatches here—they are few and far between. You'll catch the trout on scud and other aquatic-insect patterns. You can reach this small but highly productive spring run off SR 174.

Falling Spring Branch Creek
Rating: 8
Delayed Harvest regulations; Heritage Angling area; some great
hatches, and some private water in the Heritage Angling area.
DeLorme page 90, A-3 and 4

In the introduction I mentioned my first trip to Falling Spring Branch with
Barry Beck and Vince Marinaro. I never thought this creek would become
one of my favorites, but it has.

To prepare for this book I fished with Mark Sturtevant, an outdoor
writer for the *Chambersburg Public Opinion* newspaper and a director in
the Falling Spring Greenway. In addition to writing a weekly column,
Mark is a professional fly fisher. When I broke my arm I had to depend on
Mark to fish this stream one morning within the Chambersburg city lim-
its while I wrote about it. Thanks to landowners who live along the stream
the state has designated this section as a Delayed Harvest section. Yet Mark
tells me that some of the anglers who fish this section after June 15 still kill
trout. What a shame.

Despite its sometimes difficult trout, a novice can quickly capitalize
on Falling Spring. A woman named Valerie Pritchett, of WHTM news,
wanted to develop a story about fly fishing for the television station and
met Mark and me at the stream. She had never fly fished before, but within
a half hour she had missed several trout—merely a technical matter, not a
fish problem.

Much of the improvement in Falling Spring in recent years goes to the
efforts of the Greenway Association. They have done much to secure access
to the stream. Their basic premise is to work with other groups and
organizations like the Falling Spring Chapter of Trout Unlimited, the
Northern Virginia Chapter of Trout Unlimited, the Western Pennsylvania
Conservancy, the Conservation Fund, and other groups and organizations.
Basically the Greenway tries to protect, preserve, and restore the stream
while attempting to include as many people in the community as possible.

When I think of highly productive limestone streams with a good number of intense, concentrated hatches, I think first of Falling Spring Branch. But that was a decade or more ago. Something has affected the intensity of the hatches on this stream. The stream is a small one—in most areas it's not more than 20 feet wide. At one time this limestone stream boasted some spectacular hatches including Blue-Winged Olives, Tricos, Sulphurs and Yellow Drakes. Thirty-five years ago when I first fished this water the Trico hatch was spectacular and I seldom encountered another fly fisher in a morning of Trico fishing. Since that time sedimentation and urban development have diminished the intensity of the Tricos considerably, and three, four, or five other anglers might fish this much diminished spinner fall. The pressure is on.

If you are like me and you sometimes become frustrated with small hatches and matching them, then plan to fish Falling Spring evenings from mid-May through much of June. This is the time of the Sulphur hatches. Almost like clockwork you will see both Sulphur duns and spinners appearing on or over the stream around 8:30 P.M. Again, the intensity of the

When you get frustrated trying to match small hatches, head for the Sulphur hatch on Falling Spring Branch in mid-May to June.

Sulphur hatch has lessened recently. Little Blue-Winged Olives that emerge in April on this stream often can be imitated with a size-16 or size-18 pattern. To match those appearing in the fall you should use a size-20 Little Blue-Winged Olive Dun.

This limestone stream begins near the small hamlet of Falling Spring with a typical limestone spring. It flows northwest through the city of Chambersburg before it enters the Conococheague Creek. You'll find good fishing throughout the seven miles this fertile limestone streams flows. Much of the water is open to fishing because of fantastic land owners and the Greenway Association. Please respect owners' rights and thank them for allowing you to fish on private waters.

You'll also find two specially regulated fishing sections on the creek. First, there is a Heritage Angling area near the upper end off Edwards and Garman Avenues. Valley Quarries has provided parking space for fly fishers along Quarry Road. There is about a mile of private water above Garman Avenue. Above the private water you can fish in the Greenway Meadow and the Upper Greenway Meadow. Second, there is a Delayed Harvest section in Chambersburg. You can access to the upper end off U.S. 30 on Falling Spring Road which roughly parallels the stream. You can reach the lower end in Chambersburg at 7th and Montgomery Streets.

I began fishing this stream in earnest when I was a young man. How bad did I have the fishing fever? Well, in my early career I supervised the Continuing Education program at the Mont Alto Campus of Penn State University. One day I came off the stream late for a meeting with Clyde Johnson, the Director of Continuing Education. I got to campus, rushed into his office and sat down, pen and pad in hand. Clyde looked at me, looked away, looked back, and said, "Charlie, this isn't a formal meeting. You can take off the hip waders."

Green Spring Creek
Rating: 6
Delayed Harvest, fly-fishing only area.
DeLorme page 77, C-5

Green Spring is probably one of the least known and fished of the south-central Pennsylvania limestone streams. It gets little notice even though it boasts a good fish population (albeit many planted trout) because it is difficult to fish. The stream holds plenty of aquatic weeds and getting a fairly long drift in any of the numerous glides will test even the finest caster. Further, casting can be a challenge as fields high with burdock and thistles seem to reach out and capture every fly. If you can overcome these difficulties, however, then you have a shot at catching plenty of trout.

Green Spring begins near the hamlet by the same name and flows northeast along SR 641. Just below SR 641 Bulls Head Branch joins Green Spring. Green Spring flows for about five miles before it enters Conodoguinet Creek. The best area to fish is downstream from SR 641. Here you'll find weed-covered fields and a weed-choked stream with some open channels. This is the specially regulated area.

Green Spring holds the common limestone stream hatches like the Little Blue-Winged Olive and Sulphur.

Letort Spring Run
Rating: 8
A classic limestone with a Heritage Angling section.
DeLorme page 77, C-7

Of all the limestone streams mentioned in this book, Letort Spring Run has the most memories of the past for me and for many other devoted fly fishers. The love and mystique of fishing limestone streams began here many years ago. This is the stream that most of the Pennsylvania notables fished frequently. Vince Marinaro and Charlie Fox used to sit and plan daily strategies to fool these elusive brown trout. Ed Shenk and Ed Koch wrote about their experiences here. You will find markers commemorating these details. The Letort has seen it all.

But the 20- to 30-foot-wide, weed-lined Letort is one of the most difficult streams in the nation to fly fish. Often, only the middle current is weed-free. If there is no hatch (and that is frequent) catching trout here

Good casting that can overcome the heavy cover of Green Spring will be rewarded with numerous, eager trout.

can be even more difficult than on the Delaware River. But this is one stream you must fish. Consider yourself lucky and talented if you land a few trout in a day of fishing—these are sacred trout from the great Letort Spring Run.

When the Sulphur emerges you'll find trout feeding on the hatch and the concomitant spinner fall. The stream flows through the city of Carlisle in south-central Pennsylvania and empties into Conodoguinet Creek just northeast of Carlisle. You'll find a one-and-a-half-mile-long Heritage Angling area designated from 300 feet below the LR 481 bridge to the railroad bridge.

Despite its great past, though, this famous limestone water faces a troublesome future. Recent urbanization and the building of a "mega" home-supply store very close by one section of the Letort increases the risk of sedimentation and toxic-run off. How effective we are at preserving streams will be put to the test here.

Middle Spring

Rating: 5

A fair Trico hatch in the summer in open areas.

DeLorme page 77, D-4

I last fished Middle Spring Creek more than five years ago, but I still vividly remember the trip. That day I arrived at the stream in late May and saw a great Sulphur hatch. In just about every pool I fished several trout rose for the struggling duns. Recently, I went back to the same area where I hit the Sulphur hatch. I like this area of the stream. It's the lower bridge, the one at Stonewall and McClays Mill Roads. I arrived on the stream early in the morning to see if Middle Spring held a Trico hatch. A late evening thunderstorm the night before had muddied the water, but still hundreds of mating Trico spinners moved horizontally upstream and downstream in their characteristic mating flight. Even under the poorest of conditions two trout took my spent Trico pattern that morning.

Middle Spring begins just south of Shippensburg then flows north through the town and five miles later it empties into Conodoguinet Creek. State Route 696 roughly parallels the stream.

Rowe Run

Rating: 6

A classic limestone stream in the Pinola area.

DeLorme page 76, D-4

Mark Sturtevant first told me about this south-central Pennsylvania limestone stream. He said it was a classic one, but that it depended on state stocking for its supply of trout. As I traveled north of Chambersburg about fifteen miles and along SR 433 I became enamored of its look of a typical highly productive limestone stream—plenty of watercress and aquatic weeds, a cool temperature in late July, and some hatches to boot. Rowe Run seemingly has all the attributes of a great limestone stream.

But that's only one half of the picture of Rowe Run, and the other half doesn't bode well for its future. Throughout its entire drainage Rowe Run flows through open farmland, past grazing cattle and barbwire fences, and thus there is a sedimentation problem. Access to the stream is good at several locations but almost non-existent at others. Parking is limited.

This 20- to 30-foot-wide limestone stream reminds me in various stretches of Big Spring twenty-five miles to the northeast. There is a total of about five miles of water with some good hatches. Rowe Run holds some Little Blue-Winged Olives, Sulphurs and Tricos. With a reduction in sediment entering the stream I firmly believe the hatches would be heavier.

Rowe Run is in desperate need of a sponsor—Trout Unlimited or Federation of Fly Fishers club that will devote time and energy to it. Some work has already been accomplished on grazing and access by a local Boy

Scout group, but more remains to be done. With some help Rowe Run could be a fantastic trout stream. Any volunteers?

Spring Run
Rating: 5
A very small, private limestone stream.
DeLorme page 76, C-2

Recently I watched my friend Andrew Krouse fish a south-central Pennsylvania limestone stream, Spring Run, in the town of the same name. I have known Andrew for more than a decade. We first met on a freestone stream, Little Pine Creek. Then, and now, he was a consummate spinner fisher. In an average year Andrew fishes more than a hundred trout streams in the Commonwealth, and many of them are limestone waters. Last year he caught trout in more than seventy streams. Several years ago Andrew fished every specially regulated water in the state. On some streams, he considers a catch of sixty trout a good day. In an hour of fishing, he caught and released three wild brown trout on Spring Run.

Spring Run is a small, mostly private, extremely difficult limestone stream flowing in northern Franklin County. It will call upon all your casting and mending skills. Your tactics will have to be right on with the Sulphur and Trico hatches. Before you fish this stream ask the landowner for permission. And don't kill any of these beautiful wild brown trout.

Like Andrew, a number of my trout-fishing buddies are spinner fishermen who catch and release hundreds of trout every year. Fly fishermen should have nothing but admiration for other skilled anglers. A survey conducted by Penn State University and the Pennsylvania Fish and Boat Commission indicated that less than 20 percent of state anglers considered themselves fly fishers. So those of us who cast flies are really in the minority. Yet all anglers must speak with one voice to protect and restore our valuable fishing waters. Our methods may vary, but our sport is the same.

Yellow Breeches

Rating: 8

Catch-and-release water; good hatches throughout the season; heavily fished; posted land.

Page 77, D-6 and 7

My son more than a decade ago fished the Yellow Breeches Creek a mile downstream from the popular fly fishing area at Allenberry. Bryan used a tandem with a Bead Head Pheasant Tail as his wet fly. He fished directly across from two bait fishermen who hadn't caught a trout all morning. In a few minutes Bryan landed his first trout, a stocked one. In no time at all he netted four trout. This was too much for these bait fisherman and they said to Bryan after he caught his fifth trout, "There's a designated fly stretch upstream a mile—why don't you go up there and fish?"

Yellow Breeches is one of the more famous trout streams in the East. It has a specially regulated area at Allenberry which thousands of anglers frequent each year. That area, at the town of Boiling Spring, receives plenty of planted trout and holds some spectacular hatches.

Probably the best known hatch of the season on this 60-foot-wide stream is the White Fly. The White Fly appears from mid-August through early September and it brings hordes of anglers to the Yellow Breeches. Just like the Sulphur on Spring Creek and the Green Drake on Penns Creek, the White Fly on the Breeches creates a carnival-like atmosphere. Anglers assemble along the stream hours before the evening hatch discussing fishing strategies, flies, and where they plan to fish. When the hatch begins on the Breeches, around 8 or 8:30 P.M. anglers crowd in on each other and cast to a dozen or more trout taking emerging nymphs and sucking in White Fly duns.

Try to fish this prize water at a time other than when the White Fly appears. Yellow Breeches holds plenty of other hatches with less angling pressure than the White Fly hatch.

The productive White Fly hatch draws a crowd on the Yellow Breeches in mid-August to early September.

SOUTHEASTERN PENNSYLVANIA

Cedar Creek—Donegal Creek—Lititz Run—Little Bushkill Creek—
Little Lehigh Creek—Monacacy Creek—Quittapahilla Creek—
Saucon Creek—Tulpehocken Creek—Valley Creek

The heavily urbanized Allentown, Easton, Bethlehem, Reading, Lancaster, and Lebanon areas of southeastern Pennsylvania hold some surprisingly productive limestone streams. In this area you'll find well known limestone streams like the Little Lehigh, Monacacy, Little Bushkill, Tulpehocken, and Saucon Creeks. There are also many lesser known limestone streams in the area. Thanks to the foresight of past authorities sections of many of these waters in southeastern Pennsylvania flow through city, county, and state parks. These parks remain the salvation of southeastern Pennsylvania limestone fishing.

Cedar Creek

Rating: 5

A small limestone that holds a Trico hatch in the park.

DeLorme page 67, D-6

Cedar Creek gets no respect, mainly due to the fact that it flows only a few miles away from the much better known Little Lehigh. But Cedar is worth a try.

Cedar Creek flows through a city park called the Cedar Creek Parkway. In this area the stream has little vertical drop, very shallow pools, and riffles. If you can find a fairly deep area you'll find trout. Bob Toolan guided Bill King and me downstream about a half mile to the Ott Street Bridge where there is some deep water and we saw more than a dozen trout feed on various minutia. Bob tied on one fly after another for Bill and nothing seemed to work on that hot August day. Finally I suggested that Bill try a Cream Glo Bug. Yes, I hate to admit it, but a Cream Glo Bug will catch these limestone trout. On the second cast, after a half hour of nothing, Bill caught a trout on that darned fly—a beautiful 13-inch holdover brown trout that he released.

You can reach the stream off Cedar Crest Boulevard. Turn right onto Parkway Drive then right on West 30th Street. Here you'll find the Allentown Recreation Department and the Cedar Creek Parkway, and plenty of open area for fishing. But you have to contend with other park users: waders, dogs, hikers, and joggers. In this area the stream is exceedingly shallow and only 15 to 20 feet wide. If you turn left on Parkway Drive you'll reach another open area with access, the Haines Mills parking area. West Hamilton Street gets you to the Cedar Creek Park area.

Donegal Creek
Rating: 6
Delayed Harvest, fly-fishing only area.
DeLorme page 79, D-5

Don Whitesel illustrated the first edition of my book, *Trout Streams and Hatches of Pennsylvania*, with very realistic depictions of mayflies. He also introduced me to Donegal Creek in 1988. Donegal is a relatively small, isolated limestone stream in western Lancaster County. The Donegal Chapter of Trout Unlimited has diligently worked on Donegal Creek and

Lititz Run. You'll see the signs explaining their work on the lower end of the Delayed Harvest section.

Donegal holds a few of the common limestone hatches like Tricos and Sulphurs and a few other species. You can reach this 20- to 35-foot-wide limestone stream off SR 772 below Mt. Joy. You'll find the Delayed Harvest section just south of SR 772. To reach the lower end take SR 23 or Long Lane and then Donegal Creek Road. Around SR 23 the stream holds a heavy canopy. It opens up a half mile upstream. As with Lititz Run, parking along the stream is at a premium.

Lititz Run
Rating: 8
Catch-and-release water; this one is a rising star thanks to the Donegal Chapter of Trout Unlimited.
DeLorme page 79, C-7

Lititz Run holds some Sulphurs and Little Blue-Winged Olive Duns, and some hefty trout. When no hatch appears, Fred Bridge, of York, uses a Pink Worm on Lititz Run, and he catches a lot of trout with that pattern. Remember, this is a voluntary catch-and-release water, but I'd recommend that you volunteer your fish to the creek every time. Lititz is 15 to 20 feet wide and holds some deep runs. You can reach the upper end at Warwick Township Riparian Park on SR 772. To reach the project water and see the work done by the local Trout Unlimited chapter take Owl Hill Road to Millport Road to Creek Road. If you plan to fish this section you'll be hard pressed to find parking.

Lititz Run flows about four miles before it enters the Conestoga River near Millport. You'll read more about this revitalized Lancaster County limestone stream in chapter 7.

Little Bushkill Creek
Rating: 7
Catch-and-release water; a good stream in a metropolitan area.

Rich Keesler is one of the finest fly fishers in southeastern Pennsylvania. He fishes the Little Bushkill near Easton on a frequent basis. He began using the tandem rig on that stream ten years ago and he continues to use it for the phenomenal Trico and Little Blue-Winged Olive hatches here.

The Little Bushkill begins near Pen Argyl and flows south about fifteen miles before it enters the Delaware River in Easton. For an urban water this 30- to 50-foot-wide limestone stream holds some great hatches and plenty of trout. You'll find a regulated area near Easton at the Binney and Smith property.

One of the heaviest hatches of the year is the Trico. The hatch begins in June and often continues through much of October. The spinner fall is extremely dependable on this water. State Route 191 parallels much of the upper end of this fine limestone stream and SR 2019 the lower end.

Little Lehigh Creek
Rating: 8
Delayed Harvest, fly-fishing only area; Heritage Angling area; one of the greatest Trico hatches, but heavily fished.
DeLorme page 67, D-6

Little Lehigh Creek is a spectacular stream. Much of its flow will forever be open to the public for some fantastic matching-the-hatch fishing because part of this famous limestone stream runs through a city park. But you will find plenty of angling pressure—anglers flock daily to the Little Lehigh to fly fish. You'll also encounter hikers, runners, and others using the same area.

Despite its location in the urban sprawl of the southeast, the Little Lehigh boasts plenty of hatches throughout the year. With each you'll see even more anglers on the water. When the Trico appears anglers begin congregating around 6 A.M. The Trico spinner fall is fairly heavy, but the trout grow extremely selective. And well they should because each and every trout sees hundreds of Tricos patterns in any given year.

You can reach this 50-foot-wide limestone off Cedar Crest Boulevard (SR 29). If you want to get away from the angling crowds try the area

Little Lehigh Creek, one of Pennsylvania's most outstanding limestones, offers lots of hatches and excellent access.

around the Police Academy. You'll find this section about three-quarters of a mile below Bogert's Bridge. Bogert's Bridge is that high bridge you see when you fish in the Heritage Angling area. This doesn't seem to get the pressure the section upstream receives.

You'll find several Little Blue-Winged Olives on this stream along with a late summer Hex hatch. And don't forget midges. These small flies fall in the thousands on this stream almost daily. Look for trout rising to midges on almost every winter afternoon. The few times I've tried the Zebra Midge on the Little Lehigh it caught several of these highly selective trout.

Monocacy Creek
Rating: 7
Trophy-trout area; preserved by a park; holds a decent Trico hatch.
DeLorme page 68, C-1; page 67, C-7

While on a trip with me to Monocacy Creek at Illick's Mill Road access, my friend Dave Herold confessed, "I don't know how many times I've come here and tied on a dozen different patterns before I found the right one." He has fished for twenty years and knows the Monocacy well. Like me, he has come to terms with how tricky it can be, and how good: One evening during our trip, in the middle of August, he caught seven trout on a size-20 Adams.

That same evening, Dave seined the weeds in the stream and showed me some of the scuds that trout rely on here as a main staple in their diet. He often uses a scud pattern on the Monocacy when hatches aren't active. However, I've fished over trout rising to Trico spinners as early as late June.

If it weren't for those limestone aquifer streams like Monocacy and the Cedar, then the Little Lehigh and the Little Bushkill wouldn't nearly be the quality streams they are today. The Monocacy ranges from 30 to 40 feet wide in the Illick's Mill area. It begins near the hamlet of Chapman and essentially flows south emptying into the Lehigh River in Bethlehem. State Routes 987 and 512 parallel much of the upper end, SR 191 the middle section, and SR 512 gets you to part of the lower end of this fine Northampton County limestone stream. State Route 512, Center Street, parallels much of the lower half of the stream. Other access areas include Macada Road, Bridle Path Road and Monocacy Meadow Park. The latter access is near U.S. 22.

Tricking the trout in Monocacy Creek is a test of determination and skill, but you'll be a better angler for it.

Quittapahilla Creek
Rating: 7
Delayed Harvest, artificials-only section; a great recovering limestone stream.
DeLorme page 79, B-5

I first fished Quittapahilla Creek on one foggy, dreary day in late July. Rain fell the evening before but the stream still flowed clear. As I drove downstream on Syner Road to the intersection of Stelltown Road I stopped at the bridge to check for Tricos. There in a spiderweb I saw four or five struggling Trico duns. When I peered downstream I already saw the characteristic Trico mating formation over the stream. I quickly headed back upstream to the Delayed Harvest section in Annville to fish the hatch. The Tricos fell, but I had only limited success, though this remains one of the top hatches on this limestone stream.

Quittapahilla Creek flows west through Annville and empties into the Swatara Creek at Valley Glen. The 30- to 50-foot-wide stream has recently recovered from chemical spills. The state has designated almost a mile of regulated water in the town of Annville. U.S. 422 gets you close to the upper end and Syner Road to the lower end. The best fly fishing is near Annville.

Saucon Creek
Rating: 7
Selected harvest; a sleeper stream.
DeLorme page 68, D-1

There is more in southeast Pennsylvania than just the Little Lehigh, and some streams are much less crowded. Saucon Creek, flowing through Hellertown, is one of those often overlooked waters.

Saucon begins near Coopersburg and flows northeast until it empties into the Lehigh River at Bethlehem. This 20- to 40-foot-wide creek holds good Trico and Sulphur hatches along with several excellent caddisfly and

With its easy access and semi-urban setting, Saucon Creek gets a lot of weekend anglers, so try it during the week.

stonefly hatches. Thanks to the creation of Saucon Park, it will be forever open to all who want to fish. You can reach the park off SR 412 and then via Millside Drive.

"It's urban fishing at its best," my fishing friend Bill King says. Bill and his friend and guide, Bob Toolan, fished with me for a couple hours one morning in mid-August. Bob is the manager for Joe DeMarkis' Old Lehigh Outfitters (610-332-0450). Bill landed a heavy holdover trout and missed several more. Bob suggested to me that I fish the stream during the week because weekends often bring heavy angling crowds. The stream holds plenty of holdover trout in the Delayed Harvest area and some wild brown trout in its upper end near Bingen.

Tulpehocken Creek
Rating: 8
Delayed Harvest, artificials-only area; trout are highly selective and reject patterns quickly.
DeLorme page 80, B-2 and B-3

What happens when a limestone stream, or for that matter any stream, gets too much fishing pressure? The fish become highly selective. The Tulpehocken is one of these. I have been frustrated on this water more times than I care to recount. The 50- to 100-foot-wide modified tailwater is easily accessibility to thousands of anglers in southeastern Pennsylvania. State Route 3051 gets you to the upper end of this six-mile-long tailwater formed by Blue Marsh Lake. There are plenty of access points from Reber's Bridge at the upper end to the Covered Bridge downstream a few miles. One other troublesome point about the Tulpehocken: the water does warm considerably on hot summer days. Blue March Lake is rather shallow and this prevents the tailwater from becoming a true cool tailwater.

With the heavy angling pressure the trout become highly selective incredibly quickly, so use the finest fluorocarbon leader possible and the smallest fly you can cast. For example, during a Trico spinner fall on the Tulpehocken, veteran anglers use a size-26 Trico pattern rather than a size 24 to trick these finicky trout (see chapter 5 for tactics).

Valley Creek
Rating: 6
A great trout stream preserved because of Valley Forge National Park.
DeLorme page 81, D-7

Shortly after I had written about Penns Creek in *Trout Streams and Hatches of Pennsylvania* I received a letter from Andrew Leitzinger. If you read the section on Penns Creek then you already know about Andrew. I consider him a dedicated, highly skilled fly fisher. Andrew has lived in the greater Philadelphia area for the past twenty years. In that time he has fished many of the area streams and found a few with a good quantity of wild brown trout. He has even seen some Green Drakes on southeastern Pennsylvania trout streams.

One of the streams Andy speaks of most fondly is Valley Creek in Valley Forge National Park. There is a total of about four miles of open water; two miles of that total flow through the Valley Forge National Park. You can find good fishing from the park upstream past Chester Brook.

This limestone stream is truly an anomaly. Despite urban sprawl, added siltation, new parking lots, and other tremendous upstream development, Valley Creek's trout population seems fairly stable. Andy said that he used to catch occasional brook and rainbow trout a few years back, but now it is mainly stream-bred brown trout.

To reach Valley Creek get off the Valley Forge exit of the Pennsylvania Turnpike and take U.S. 202 south to SR 252 north. The stream is a delight to fish and a short drive from the bright lights of Philadelphia.

3

Select Limestone Streams of Maryland and Virginia

MARYLAND

Look at the geologic map of Maryland and you'll see a twenty- to thirty-mile-wide swath from north to south of limestone bedrock, mainly in central Washington County. That karst region is home to a once neglected and overlooked stream, Beaver Creek. But Beaver Creek is making a valiant attempt to come back to what it once was.

Beaver Creek
Rating: 6
Catch-and-release water; should become better in a few years.
DeLorme (PA) page 90, D-4

"Once in Maryland, I was fishing Beaver Creek, a small limestone stream." That quote comes from Joe Brook's great book, *The Complete Book of Fly Fishing*. Joe and other famous writers often wrote about this stream in the late 1950s. Why shouldn't they have? The stream teemed with healthy wild trout. A true limestone with a huge spring at its origin, the Beaver boasted a good number of hatches. But something happened to Beaver Creek in the 1970s. Sedimentation, degradation caused by cattle, deforestation, and chemical sprays all seemed to decimate the stream's trout and their food. "No Trespassing" signs and no fishing became the norm.

Enter the Beaver Creek Watershed Association in 2002. This group of landowners and others, along with a great deal of help from the Chesapeake Bay Foundation, the Federation of Fly Fishers, and Trout Unlimited, began to work on this forgotten, diminished limestone stream. The Watershed Association focused on stream stabilization, reforestation, stream improvement, and fishing access. Each and every day the association declares a workday the Chesapeake Bay Foundation supplies dozens of volunteers. These volunteers and the Foundation have added considerably to the bright future of this stream. Within a few years this stream has made a 180-degree turn. The outlook for this once neglected limestone fishery is highly encouraging.

The association found funds to work on stream improvements. They now have a one-mile stretch of this cool limestone designated as a catch-and-release area. They have also developed two parking lots open to fly fishers. And they are presently working on another 1,000-foot section of the river, just below Black Rock Creek. Their far-ranging projects include reforestation of an upper open section of the creek, fencing in cattle to protect the banks along the stream, and much more.

Beaver Creek is becoming what it once was back in the 1950s—a topnotch, cold-water fishery.

With all its advocates, the Beaver is another example of what can happen when diverse organizations and people become involved in a single cause. For example, Mike Steiner, owner of a golf course; Elmer Wibley, of the Washington County Soil District; Charles Jackson and Mike Macguire, non-fishing landowners; and Doug Hutzell, leader of the restoration—all have taken a deep interest in Beaver Creek's total recovery.

But unless these trout have any significant type of food the restoration process is futile. Luckily for Beaver Creek it holds Sulphurs, Little Blue-Winged Olives, March Browns, a Hex hatch and plenty of scuds and crayfish.

Much of this 30- to 50-foot-wide limestone in the catch-and-release area contains a heavy canopy and fishing at many places is difficult if not downright impossible. Recently Mark Sturtevant and Mike Saylor accompanied me on a fishing trip on Beaver Creek. At the lowest section of the catch-and-release area Mark had a half dozen trout rising in front of him—in the middle of the afternoon and in late July. As he worked his way upstream casting to trout he missed four of them before he landed his first rainbow. Mike told us that the week before he landed a trout over 15 inches long in this same stretch.

Beaver Creek holds some wild browns and planted browns and rainbows. Additionally the state has designated some wild brown trout from the Gunpowder River for stocking in the stream.

There's about thirteen miles of total stream. You can access Beaver Creek by taking Interstate 70 to U.S. Route 40 East. Take Beaver Creek Road to Cool Hollow Road to the stream. You'll find an access parking area just south.

VIRGINIA
Beaver Creek–Mossy Creek–North River
Travel south on I-81 through western Virginia and you will view some spectacular scenery. To the west stands the Allegheny Mountains and the George Washington National Forest. To the east in the far distance you will see the awe-inspiring Blue Ridge Mountains, the Shenandoah National Park, and Skyline Drive. Between the majestic mountains lies the nearly fifty-mile-wide Shenandoah Valley. This expansive valley holds deposits of limestone and in turn great trout fishing on limestone streams. Around Harrisonburg you will encounter the likes of Beaver Creek, Mossy Creek, and the North River.

Beaver Creek
Rating: 8
Catch-and-release, fly-fishing only area; a great little limestone stream with plenty of hatches.
DeLorme page 66, A-3

Brian Trow and I hit this small limestone stream in the middle of August around noon. Mid-August is no time to search for the qualities of a fine limestone stream. The Trico had already ended for the day and no further hatches would occur until evening. But in front of us, within sight of the Ottobine Elementary School, in a deep pool and riffle, Brian and I saw more than a dozen rainbows feed freely off the surface. We tried to determine what food source these fish found, but that we couldn't see anything on the surface or in the air. Was it a midge, a beetle, or an extremely small mayfly? Brian and I thought of each possibility, discarding most as implausible. Finally it came to us: These fish fed on small winged ants. Late August in the East brings great numbers of winged ants to the water. These same terrestrials appear in Pennsylvania like clockwork every year around August 25.

Brian tied on a size-20 ant pattern and began casting to a pod of risers. We quickly knew that we had made the right choice. On the second or third cast a small rainbow hit. It looked like a wild fish. Several more casts brought in a larger rainbow, and on and on for the next two hours. Brian caught and released more than a dozen trout and missed many others.

We had fabulous fishing on a hot August afternoon, worth every ounce of perspiration. Beaver Creek is one of my small-stream favorites in the East.

Guide Brian Trow shows off a pretty little rainbow trout on Beaver Creek, a stream that is undergoing a complete resurrection.

Although Beaver and Mossy Creeks flow just a few miles apart they are incredibly dissimilar in character. Mossy is a weed-filled, slowly moving stream that is fairly difficult to fly fish. Beaver Creek, on the other hand, is an atypical limestone with plenty of gradient and therefore many riffles and pools. It even seems less influenced by agriculture. Beaver is much easier to fly fish.

You'll find about two miles of open water on Beaver Creek. You must obtain a permit to fly fish on the stream. You can get one from Doug Michael at the Ottobine Country Store or Billy Kingsley at Blue Ridge Anglers in Harrisonburg. Four permits are available per day and you must make a contribution, usually $5. The money goes to a good cause: the Massanutten Chapter of Trout Unlimited. This latter organization oversees the two-mile fishing area.

Beaver holds plenty of rainbows, a few browns, and some brook trout; some of these are planted, some holdovers, and some stream bred. On that hot August afternoon Brian caught a half dozen rainbows that were less than 4 inches long. They all looked like wild fish.

Beaver is easy to access. Take State Route (SR) 257 out of Bridgewater about ten miles to reach the stream. Once on the stream, watch out for electric fences.

Beaver holds plenty of hatches. It holds some Green Drakes, Sulphurs and a good Trico hatch throughout the summer. On that hot afternoon we even saw some larger dark gray mayflies emerge that looked Slate Drakes. We couldn't capture one, so I was unable to identify the mayfly.

Dry River produces the water that eventually becomes Beaver Creek. Beaver, Mossy, and Spring Creeks empty into the North River within a half mile and this plus some springs produce some good fishing on the North River.

Mossy Creek
Rating: 9
Can keep one trout, 20 inches or longer; a classic limestone stream with plenty of hatches.
DeLorme page 66, B-3

Thousands of size-24 and size-26 Little Blue-Winged Olives began emerging at 6:30 P.M. as Brian and Colby Trow approached this small, cold, fertile limestone stream. Yes, this is a productive limestone stream and I know it is supposed to have some spectacular hatches—just not in mid-August, and not in the evening at that time. But this is Mossy Creek, and some believe it to be a miniature insect factory. In 2004, *Field and Stream* rated Mossy Creek at Number 5 on its list of spring creeks nationwide.

Brian and Colby Trow fish Mossy several times a week. They claim that it is an important part of their operating procedure because they run Mossy Creek Fly Fishing, an Orvis dealership on U.S. 33 East in Harrisonburg, Virginia (mossycreekflyfishing.com). The fraternal twins are only 25 years old but they are more than 50 in fishing years. At 13, the two gave fly-tying demonstrations at the Virginia Fly Fishing Federations meetings; Colby ties an intricate wiggle-frog pattern that is unbelievably realistic. The Fly Fishers of Virginia changed its rules to allow the two teenagers to enter the organization.

Beautiful, meandering Mossy Creek was selected by *Field and Stream* magazine as one of the country's top 10 spring creeks.

This Mossy Creek brown trout fell for a beetle pattern fished by Virginia guide Colby Trow.

The time we fished on Mossy Creek, Brian tried a terrific beetle pattern that Jim Finn ties for the fly shop. On the second or third cast a small trout violently struck the terrestrial. Brian and Colby fish that beetle pattern just downstream from some of the sycamores that line the stream because they found that thousands of Japanese beetles feed on the leaves of these trees. On one cast on our way upstream, Brian slapped the beetle pattern loudly on the surface and a dark brown trout dashed downstream a couple feet to grab the pattern. The two brothers landed four trout in an hour of fishing that evening and missed many more.

Mossy is not for the angler with little casting experience. Its trees, bushes, thistles, and weed beds will test even the most experienced fly fisher. But, the experience is still worth it.

Mossy Creek holds plenty of trout though it gets heavy angling pressure almost daily. The state annually plants 10,000 trout in the four miles of open water. These planted trout, plus plenty of holdovers and some wild fish, give Mossy Creek its great numbers. These fingerlings grow quickly in this food factory. You can encounter dozens of rising trout every day.

In addition to the Little Blue-Winged Olive Dun that we encountered that August evening, Mossy has plenty of other food. The stream boasts a great number of Sulphurs in May and June, and hosts daily a highly fishable Trico hatch and spinner fall from June through much of October. (Brian and Colby tell me that they have even heard of fishable hatches of Tricos into late November. Both recommend a Jim Finn pattern that has a fine abdomen of light chartreuse tying thread. This pattern works best when the female spinner falls.) Mossy even has a few Green Drakes around the third week in May. Terrestrial patterns are essential in midsummer. Local guide Bob Cramer created the Disco Cricket for the Mossy. I used that pattern back in 1992 on the stream and it still produces trout today.

With its hatches, plenty of trout, and four miles of open water, you might think Mossy Creek is the perfect limestone stream. But Mossy experiences the same pollution problems that many others do because it is positioned in the middle of agricultural land. Nitrates, bacteria and other indicators suggest that the stream is degrading or retrogressing. What is being done? The Mossy Creek Coalition, an association of conservation organizations and farmers, is trying to restore Mossy Creek to its proper place as a top limestone without the pollutants.

You must obtain a free permit from Virginia Department of Game and Inland Fisheries in Verona to fish the open water on Mossy Creek. Call them ahead of time and they will mail you a permit. Mossy Creek begins at Joseph Spring near Mt. Solon. You'll find two parking areas. The lower parking lot is located at SR 42 and Iron Works Road. There are plenty of trout in this lower section, but the bushes, trees, and other vegetation will test even the best fly caster. You'll find the other parking lot upstream a couple miles on SR 42.

I mentioned Bob Cramer several times. He's a member of the Mossy Creek Coalition (bobcramer.com). When I prepared *Great Rivers—Great Hatches* back in 1992 I fished on Mossy Creek with Bob. He is the only Orvis-endorsed guide in Virginia. He is also a tremendous fly fisher, guide, and fly tier, and he knows every inch of water on Mossy Creek. Bob, Colby, and Brian guide on the local limestone streams, the Shenandoah

River for smallmouth bass, and small brook trout streams in the Blue Ridge Mountains. Bob also guides on a private section of Mossy Creek.

North River
Rating: 7
Mostly private with some big fish.
DeLorme page 66, A-3

North River and Smith Creek are mainly private waters. The North River begins as a freestone stream in the Allegheny Mountains. Here it is stocked and becomes highly marginal in midsummer. After the river reappears out of the gorge and into the limestone valley below it loses much of its flow. This is the aquifer that supplies Mossy Creek. Mossy, Beaver, and Spring Creeks enter the North River in less than a half mile apart and just upriver from Bridgewater. These three limestones have a tremendous effect on this river and it produces some huge trout. Reports of trout over 20 inches long are common.

You can get information on fishing this river by contacting Colby and Brian Trow at Mossy Creek Fly Fishing or Billy Kingsley at Blue Ridge Anglers. Both of these fine shops are located in Harrisonburg. Billy guides on both the North River and Smith Creek.

The North, Middle, and South Rivers form the South Fork of the Shenandoah River near Grottoes.

4

Trout Food in Limestone Streams

THE BASIC FOOD GROUPS

Anglers and trout alike look forward to some of the well-known hatches that appear annually on just about every limestone stream worth its reputation. The vast majority of these streams boast impressive Sulphur hatches that appear every evening for more than two weeks. And many of these same waters host Trico spinner falls that continue uninterrupted every morning in late summer for more than two months. Some of the very best limestone streams possess ten, fifteen, and even more notable hatches every year.

Look at Big Fishing and Penns Creeks in central Pennsylvania as examples of proprietors of countless fine hatches throughout the season. On any afternoon in late April, Big Fishing Creek might display six important hatches that cater to rising trout. Early Brown Stoneflies, Grannoms, Little Blue-Winged Olive Duns, Hendricksons, Blue Quills, and Quill Gordons vie for the angler's and the trout's attention. On two occasions I have fished over trout rising to five of those hatches in the same day. In late May Big Fishing Creek again comes alive with Sulphurs, Green Drakes, and Slate Drakes—all appearing in the evening. The same hatching activity goes for Penns Creek and dozens of other highly productive limestone streams.

The more hatches a stream holds, the more opportunities you have to catch trout actively feeding, and the more decisions you have to make about

The mighty Green Drake, one of the largest mayflies in the East and the cause of much elbow-to-elbow fishing.

what pattern to use and how to handle situations of high angling pressure. On multiple-hatch days trout often switch from feeding on one hatch to another, and you're going to have to be able to react to that. When more famous streams are jam-packed during the Sulphur, Green Drake, and Trico hatches, you might want to select a lesser-known stream to fish or select a part of the famous stream that doesn't get as much pressure. Even with the heavy pressure matching, the hatches on these waters are extremely important.

Hatch activity and the trout feeding on those insects are similar to the artificial feeding setup at fish hatcheries and much can be gained by watching trout in a controlled situation. The trout go crazy and eat greedily on their supply of trout pellets, losing all timidity and feeding undisturbed. On many private streams where trout are too plentiful and don't have enough natural food, owners sometimes feed them pellets in the stream. (I've seen anglers on those streams resort to an imitation of the trout pellet as a fly and catch many trout.) The same type of feeding characteristic often holds true when trout feed naturally on a river, stream, or lake. When nourishment appears, trout feed quickly and gluttonously. Beginning anglers often ask me how long it takes a stocked trout to begin feeding on naturals on the water. Believe me: trout don't take long to get acclimated. I've noted on several occasions trout

The Sulphur, an archetypal mayfly, provides some of the steadiest, most reliable hatches on limestones.

that fed on emerging insects within 15 minutes after they were planted. On Silver Creek, a spring creek in north-central Arizona, trout fed on a hatch of diminutive Blue-Winged Olives just minutes after they were released.

Chapter 6 looks at recipes for most phases of the insects you see on limestone streams. It also examines in more detail the hatching process. Fertile limestone streams often hold denser and a larger diversity of hatches than do their freestone counterparts; thus hatches like the Sulphur, Trico, Little Blue-Winged Olive Dun, and others can take on added importance on these limestone waters. We'll look at these insects in more detail later in this chapter, but first we'll examine some of the major types of food that trout eat.

Mayflies

Mayflies (order Ephemeroptera) make up a large part of most species' food. These insects are extremely common and tremendously important on limestone streams. Their scientific name, Ephemeroptera, means "ephemeral" or short lived. Mayflies live out of water one to three days and then they die. However, the larva of many mayflies lives approximately 362 days, all underwater. In the entire life cycle (the development from an egg to an egg-laying adult) trout most often eat the nymph or larva—that part of the life cycle that lives underwater.

TABLE 2: MAYFLIES COMMON ON LIMESTONE STREAMS (IN ORDER OF ANNUAL HATCH DATES)

Common Name	Scientific Name	Emergence Date	Emergence Time	Size	Remarks
Little Blue-Winged Olive Dun	*Baetis tricaudatus*	March and April; later hatch in September and October	Afternoon	16–20	One of the top three most common hatches. Look for it on inclement days.
Grannom (Caddisfly)	*Brachycentrus* genus	Mid-April to mid-May	Variable	10–16	Size varies from a size 10 or 12 on Penns Creek to a size 14 or 16 on Spruce Creek.
Speckle-Winged Dun	*Callibaetis skokianis*	April through much of the summer	Usually late morning	14–16	Look for the hatch on limestone ponds or dams as well as streams.
Blue Quill or Mahogany Dun	*Paraleptophlebia* genus	Mid-April until late October (a variety of species)	Spring hatches in the early afternoon; later hatches usually early in the morning.	16–18	
Quill Gordon	*Epeorus pleuralis*	Early April through much of May	Early afternoon	14	Look for the hatch on fast stretches of limestone streams.
Hendrickson	*Ephemerella subvaria*	April and early May	Usually in mid-afternoon	12–16	

March Brown	*Stenonema vicarium*	Second week in May until early June	Most often in the afternoon and early evening	12	These are sporadic emergers that sometimes appear on the surface in concentrated numbers near dusk.
Sulphur	*Ephemerella rotunda, invaria,* and *dorothea*	Second week in May well into June	First two days in the afternoon; then hatch moves to 8:30 P.M.	16, 18	Consistently one of the top hatches on limestone streams.
Light Cahill	*Stenacron interpunctatum*	Last week in May and through most of June	Mid-evening around 7 P.M.	12,14	Often found emerging with Sulphurs.
Blue-Winged Olive Dun	*Drunella cornuta*	End of May through much of June and early July	Late in the morning and early afternoon	14–16	
Dark Green Drake	*Litobrancha recurvata*	End of May and early June	An afternoon emerger	8–10	This big mayfly often emerges on the smaller limestone streams.
Green Drake	*Ephemera guttulata*	Mid-May until mid-June, depending on location	In late afternoon on heavily canopied streams; dusk and later on larger waters	6–12; variable depending on the size and fertility of the stream	Found on moderately flowing stretches of water, not slow, meandering limestone streams.
Slate Drake	*Isonychia bicolor*	Late May and June; September; and early October	Summer hatch around 7 P.M.; fall hatch in late afternoon	12-14; usually a size 12 in spring, size 14 in fall	Hatch is found on faster stretches of water.

(continued)

TABLE 2: MAYFLIES COMMON ON LIMESTONE STREAMS (IN ORDER OF ANNUAL HATCH DATES) *(CONTINUED)*

Common Name	Scientific Name	Emergence Date	Emergence Time	Size	Remarks
Pink Cahill	*Epeorus vitreus*	Late May and early June	Evening	14	Two separate patterns required: Light Cahill for the male; Pink Cahill for the female.
Brown Drake	*Ephemera simulans*	Late May and early June	Most often just at dusk	8–10	Hatch is very short-lived.
Cream Cahill	*Stenonema pulchellum* and *modestum*	Late May and early June	Evening	14–16	
Olive Sulphur	*Ephemerella needhami*	Early June	Sporadic in the afternoon and concentrated at dusk	16	The female has a greenish-olive body and the male a dark brown one.
Blue-Winged Olive Dun (later version)	*Drunella cornutella*	Mid-June through early July	Late morning and afternoon	16	This later Blue-Winged Olive is smaller than the earlier hatch.
Pale Evening Dun	*Ephemerella dorothea, E. septentrionalis; Heptagenia* species like *H. walshi, aphrodite*	Late May to early July	Evening	16–20	
Yellow Drake	*Ephemera varia*	Mid-June through much of July	Evening	10–12	Inhabits slower currents.
Trico	*Trico stygiatus, allectus,* and *minutus*	Late June through October	Mornings	20–24	One of the three most common hatches on limestone streams.

Blue Quill	*Paraleptophlebia guttata*	June through September	Mornings	18	Often confused with the Trico spinner.
Big Slate Drake	*Hexagenia atrocaudata*	Mid-August	Dusk	8	Common in central and southern Pennsylvania and south to Virginia.
White Fly	*Ephoron leukon*	August into early September	Evening to past dusk	14	Female remains a dun; only the male changes to a spinner.

If you have fished limestone streams very often then you probably already realize that there are two types of nymphs that frequent these waters. First and most important on many of these fertile waters are those mayfly nymphs classified as *free swimmers*. These nymphs swim freely along the bottom or cling to some aquatic weeds. But they do not burrow and only occasionally cling to rocks. Trico, Blue-Winged Olive, Sulphur, and Little Blue-Winged Olive nymphs exhibit this behavior. The second type of nymph many limestone streams hold is the *burrower*. This nymphs lives in the bottom of the streambed or substrate. The White Fly, Green Drake, Big Slate Drake, and Yellow Drake exhibit this type of existence.

A third type of nymph, the *clinger*, attaches itself to rocks, and isn't so often found in limestone streams. Pine Creek in central Pennsylvania shows why. When I fished this excellent stream, very seldom did I see a rock or log in the water. When I did find a submerged log or the occasional rock I found hundreds of mayfly nymphs attached to it. So on limestones that have less structure than their freestone counterparts, clingers (March Browns, Light Cahills, Quill Gordons, and many others) can't find enough cover; some clingers also need fast water.

I said earlier that there is often a high correlation between a heavily fished stream and the number and quality of hatches that water contains. Look at your better trout waters across the East. Show me a stream with angling pressure and I'll show you a stream with plenty of hatches. Hatch volume on limestone streams magnifies that condition.

I said earlier that great hatches produce almost a carnival-like atmosphere on various waters. If you've ever fished Penns or Yellow Creeks in Pennsylvania during the Green Drake hatch, or the Yellow Breeches when the White Fly appears, then you have seen this human phenomena. Anglers arrive as early as three or four hours before the hatch comes off and sit stream-side, chatting, slowly getting their gear ready, all in anticipation of the hatch. The Green Drake hatch on Big Fishing Creek in central Pennsylvania, the Trico on the Little Lehigh in southeastern Pennsylvania, and the Sulphur hatch on Spring Creek in central Pennsylvania are all similar affairs.

There's a rule I often follow when I want to fish one of the more noted hatches. I avoid some of the more famous streams during hatches and keep driving or walking to less well-known limestone waters that hold the same hatch. While hundreds of anglers frequent Spring Creek above and below Bellefonte, I'm fishing the same hatch just five miles downstream where I'll encounter larger water and fewer anglers. Have rod, will travel.

Stoneflies and Caddisflies

Caddisflies (order Trichoptera) and stoneflies (order Plecoptera) are similar to the mayflies in their development. Anglers often call these *down-wing* insects because of the configuration of their wings when at rest. Stoneflies and mayflies, however, lack one stage of the complete insect life cycle—the pupa stage—and are, therefore, considered to have incomplete metamorphosis. But caddisflies pass through the pupa or "resting phase." This period usually lasts several weeks. Unlike stonefly and mayfly nymphs, however, caddis larvas lack the tough outer shell, the *exoskeleton*. Therefore, some caddis (but not all) construct a protective shelter or case from small sticks or stream debris. Caddisflies can be grouped according to the type of case they build.

Stonefly nymphs take one to three years to develop, depending on the species, so fishing big nymphs for them is a key tactic. (The nymph or larva

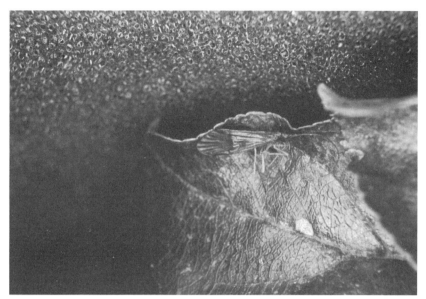

Caddisflies are also a staple of the trout's insect diet. They're often called "down-wings" because of how they fold their wings.

of all species is available to trout almost every day of the year, whereas the adult is available for only about a few days; thus, nymph fishing will usually outperform fishing dry flies when there is no hatch.) You'll see different ent sizes of Salmon Fly nymphs on western waters and Giant Stoneflies in the East because they take three years to complete their life cycle. When they do emerge, mating usually takes place while they are resting on some surface rather than while they are in flight.

Midges

Paul Needham, in his book *Trout Streams,* says, "Midge larvae and pupae are the most important single food item for trout under three inches in length." Yet one the most overlooked and underfished hatches in the East is that of the chironomid, or midge (order Diptera). These are small insects that live their larval life in the water. When they emerge, midge adults look like mosquitoes. (Mosquitoes and craneflies are also members of this two-winged family of insects.) Until a dozen years ago I used a pattern

This bug, the fishfly, isn't as well known as mayflies or stoneflies, but is good trout food just the same.

to copy these important true flies very infrequently. Now I copy these hatches often.

The midge takes on the most importance on western rivers like the San Juan in New Mexico, the Frying Pan and Cache la Poudre Rivers in Colorado, and the Missouri in Montana, and well it should.

But midges can also be extremely important on eastern limestone streams. I've seen many winter afternoons where trout fed consistently for an hour or more on those small insects. Even Spring Creek in central Pennsylvania hosts midges all winter long. Before and during the hatch I often use a size-16, size-18 or size-20 Zebra Midge. I often fish this pattern a foot deep behind a dry fly. I tie the Zebra Midge in with bodies of black, dark brown and olive tying thread.

Midges are found on just about every stream and river across the continent. Limestone streams seem to have an abundance of these. Many of our limestone streams have midge hatches almost daily. Midges are extremely important both as wet and dry fly patterns.

Limestone streams often have daily midge hatches, making this mosquito-like bug a go-to pattern when all else fails.

Craneflies

Craneflies (order Diptera) look like large mosquitoes. They can be important on limestone streams. Steve Sywensky, a noted fly tier in central Pennsylvania, fishes cranefly patterns especially on Spring Creek in central Pennsylvania through the summer. You fish these larger patterns just like a usual dry fly, but you can try skittering them too: make them skip or skate across the water. (In the early days of Catskill fly fishing, skittering spider-like patterns was a main tactic.) Craneflies come with body colors of yellow, tan, and olive.

Terrestrials

Terrestrials are landborn insects that find their way onto the water's surface. They include, but are not limited to, beetles, grasshoppers, crickets, ants, and jassids. In addition to landborn beetles there are many aquatic forms of beetles that spend their entire life underwater. Terrestrials are of special importance in June, July, and August. Trout slyly feed on these

All through the summer, landborn insects like beetles land on the water's surface, so you'll need a few patterns for your fly box.

insects near stream banks in heavily shaded stretches, but you can often detect that fish are rising to terrestrials and not flies.

Crayfish and Scuds

Crayfish (order Decapoda) and scuds (order Amphipoda) are important sources of food for trout, especially on limestone streams. These are the hidden food sources. Unlike mayflies, stoneflies, caddisflies, midges, and craneflies, these tiny animal forms don't appear on the surface. Unless you check some aquatic plants, rocks, and other sunken objects these crustaceans are out of sight. Trout can feed on decapods and amphipods any time of the year. Therefore, you should carry a good supply all year long when you fish limestone waters. Scuds, or freshwater shrimp, as many anglers call them, are an especially important source of food for trout in limestone or alkaline streams, rivers and lakes and are vital to the growth of limestone trout. Anglers have come up with excellent imitations for crayfish and scuds. You'll find some of these patterns in chapter 6.

Sow Bugs

Sow bugs (order Isopoda) on eastern limestone streams are often called cress bugs. Sow bugs crawl along vegetation (mainly watercress) very slowly and are sometimes dislodged from their homes. Their general body color is dark olive to dark gray to dark brown. There are several good patterns for this 1-inch flattened isopod. You'll find a good pattern in chapter 6.

THE MOST COMMON HATCHES

Show me a limestone stream and I'll show you one at least of five or six hatches. First and foremost, many of these streams harbor decent but tiny Tricos and Little Blue-Winged Olive Duns. Other hatches common on limestone waters include Sulphurs, Blue-Winged Olives, Speckle-Winged Duns, Green Drakes, and White Flies. What follows here is a discussion of each of these common hatches, in order of abundance, followed by a list of waters where they are found and a chart detailing hatch times and patterns.

Trico (includes *Tricorythodes allectus, Tricorythodes fictus* and *Tricorythodes minutus*)

One of the most common hatches in North America is the Trico. What it lacks in size it makes up in sheer quantity and the number of days it annually appears. But this small mayfly brings added angling pressure to a stream late in the fly-fishing season. Until a couple decades ago few anglers knew much about this diminutive mayfly. Many of the uninitiated at that time called it the *Caenis* hatch. More recently, a number of outdoor writers have extensively studied this hatch and spinner fall, especially on limestone streams. Charlie Fox, Vince Marinaro, Bob Miller, Ed Koch, and George Harvey have all written expansively about Trico fishing on Pennsylvania limestone streams.

A few years ago Bob Miller wrote a book called *Tricos*. Can you believe it—reading an entire book on one diminutive genus, *Tricorythodes*? The scope of the book is limited to just four limestone streams in southeastern

Pennsylvania but is definitely a worthwhile read about fishing this hatch on limestone streams.

The Trico hatch is probably one of the most dependable hatches of the year. If you know a stream that holds this hatch you can travel there any morning in late summer or early fall and you can be rest assured that you will see the hatch. In most areas of United States there are two generations each year. In the Southwest, near Phoenix, there are many generations and the hatch appears just about the entire year.

No matter what limestone stream you fish for trout, you will probably encounter this small mayfly in August, September, and October. Look for especially heavy hatches and spinner flights on streams with a sparse or no canopy. Mating spinners need plenty of overhead room to perform their flight. The hatch begins in June on the Monacacy Creek near Bethlehem, Pennsylvania, and Mossy Creek in Virginia, and continues well into October and early November on many southern Pennsylvania and Virginia

Tricos create some of the heaviest hatches on limestone streams, and can appear well into November.

The female Trico dun is the one you'll most likely see, as the male dun emerges at night.

limestone streams. I have fished spinner falls as late as mid-November on these waters.

Why don't you ever see the dark brown male dun emerging? A few years back Ronald Hall conducted a comprehensive study on the Trico hatch and spinner fall as part of the requirements for his doctoral degree at the University of Minnesota. He found that most male duns emerge from 10 P.M. to 2 A.M. while most female duns appear on the surface in the early morning hours, usually from 6 to 9 A.M. So if you want to see the male Trico dun you have to look for it late at night.

Hall also found several other interesting points that he spelled out about Tricos in his thesis. About forty-nine days after the first generation of Tricos lays its eggs, the second generation appears. There is much over-lapping of generations so that's why the hatch is heavy throughout late summer. The hatch has one generation per year (univoltine) in some parts of Canada, two generations each year (bivoltine) in much of the northern half of the United States, and many generations per year (multivoltine) in parts of the Southwest.

Hall found that in colder climates the Trico spends winters in the egg stage. Therefore, in many northern areas you won't find any Trico nymphs from December through much of May. Nymphs emerge from the eggs near the end of May and emerge as duns approximately fifty days later.

Hall's study gives you a total picture of the hatch and its many intricacies. After reading Hall's thesis you certainly wouldn't use a Trico Nymph before June or July—even on streams that hold this as the only major hatch. Second, if you plan to tie a pattern to copy the emerging dun then you want to imitate the pale olive female because the male emerges at night.

Sometimes anglers confuse the Trico with the summer-appearing Blue Quill (*Paraleptophlebia guttata*). Both appear on limestone streams

The Blue Quill male dun, the "Jenny Spinner," is often mistaken for a Trico—both appear at the same time, in heavy numbers.

in heavy numbers. Anglers call the male spinner of the Blue Quill the "Jenny Spinner" and the female the "Dark Brown Spinner." Both Tricos and Jenny Spinners become active at the same time and both are extremely common on limestone streams. Both species also share similar body colorations, brown and white (although opposite colors in the two sexes). However, a trained eye can distinguish the two fairly quickly in flight. The Blue Quill is a couple sizes larger than the Trico and the two male swarms form a different mating arrangement. Trico Spinners move in a horizontal plane and Jenny Spinners in a vertical one.

Beaver Creek, VA
Cedar Run, PA (Allentown area)
Clover Creek, PA
Elk Creek, PA
Falling Spring Branch, PA
Letort Spring Run, PA
Little Bushkill Creek, PA
Little Juniata River, PA (spotty)
Little Lehigh Creek, PA
Lower Bald Eagle, PA
Middle Spring, PA
Monocacy Creek, PA
Mossy Creek, VA
Penns Creek, PA (upper end)
Piney Creek, PA
Quittapahilla Creek, PA
Saucon Creek, PA
Silver Creek, ID
Spring Creek, PA
Spruce Creek, PA
Tulpehocken Creek, PA
Yellow Breeches, PA

TABLE 3: THE TRICO HATCH

Hatch	Time of Year	Special Consider-ations	Approximate Time to Fish the Dun (Female)	Approximate Time to Fish the Spinner	Pattern to Use	Remarks
Trico (various species)	June–July	Male emerges 10 P.M.– 2 A.M.; female 6–9 A.M.	6–9 A.M.	8–10 A.M.	Trico Dun Trico Spinner	Hatch usually begins in June or July in southern Pennsyl-vania and Virginia.
	August		6–8 A.M.	7–10 A.M.		
	September		6–9 A.M.	7–10 A.M.		
	October		7–11 A.M.	8–Noon		
	November		11 A.M.– 3 P.M.	10–3 P.M.		

Little Blue-Winged Olive Dun (*Baetis tricaudatus*; other closely related species that appear at the same time like *Baetis intercalaris*)

Where have I seen Little Blue-Winged Olive Dun hatches? Everywhere. Show me a good tailwater or limestone stream and I'll show you hatch of these small but important dark olive mayflies. The tailwaters of New Mexico's San Juan River holds one of the heaviest hatches. On the San Juan you can expect to see hatches almost any time of the year; but the best hatches appear in early spring and fall. One of the best hatches I ever experienced occurred on a relatively unknown spring creek in central Arizona called Silver Creek. That same diminutive hatch also inhabits just about every respectable limestone stream in the East. Probably the heaviest hatches I have experienced on limestone streams in the East occurred on Big Fishing Creek in central Pennsylvania. Even on in-

The Little Blue-Winged Olive dun, which often hatches on rainy, cooler days, appears in two generations—spring and fall.

clement days on that stream I have seen Little Blue-Winged Olive hatches last for two or three hours.

The Little Blue-Winged Olive has several things in common with the Trico. As with the Trico, the Little Blue-Winged Olive makes up for its relatively small size by the sheer numbers that emerge. And like the Trico the Little Blue-Winged Olive produces two generations each year in most areas. The early generation appears in March and April and the late generation emerges in September and October. You say that you've seen Little Blue-Winged Olives in midsummer? The common name, Little Blue-Winged Olive, represents a dozen or more different species. Many of these species appear in May, June, and July. Anglers call several genera of mayflies in the family Baetidae, like *Acentrella, Plauditus,* and *Baetis,* "Little Blue-Winged Olives." Usually one or two patterns in sizes 18 to 24 copy most of these species.

The Trico and Little Blue-Winged Olive also differ in some aspects. The dun is often the more important phase to imitate with the Little Blue-Winged Olive and the spinner is usually the more important phase in the Trico. The Trico is a morning emerger and the Little Blue-Winged Olive is often an afternoon emerger.

I can almost predict the type of day that I'll see the Little Blue-Winged Olive appear. I often call it "the lousy day hatch." I have fished Little Blue-Winged Olive hatches that have continued for hours on rainy days. Show me a cool, inclement, drizzly afternoon in April and May or September and October and I'll show you a heavy hatch of Little Blue-Winged Olives. I have seen heavy hatches on lousy days from Silver Creek in Arizona to the Little Juniata River, Falling Spring Branch, and Big Fishing Creeks in Pennsylvania. Be prepared for this hatch with plenty of size-18 and size-20 dark-olive bodied patterns. A Vernille-bodied pattern has worked well for me.

A spinner of the *Baetis* genus, one of four very similar mayfly genera all referred to commonly as "Little Blue-Winged Olives."

The Little Blue-Winged Olive is often the first mayfly to appear in the late winter/early spring time frame and one of the last to appear in fall and early winter. I have seen the hatch on limestone streams as early as mid-February and as late as mid-December.

Keep checking the insects on the water to make certain you are fishing the correct pattern. One afternoon on Big Fishing Creek I fished for more than an hour over a heavy Little Blue-Winged Olive hatch. After that hour the trout quit hitting my pattern but they continued to rise. Finally after about a half an hour of mismatching the hatch, I checked the insects on the water. I noted that only one in ten of the mayflies on the water were now Little Blue-Winged Olives. Blue Quills made up the majority of bugs. I quickly, if belatedly, tied on a size-18 Blue Quill and began catching trout again.

Beaver Creek, MD
Beaver Creek, VA
Big Fishing Creek, PA
Falling Spring Branch, PA
Letort Spring Run, PA
Little Bushkill Creek, PA
Little Juniata River, PA
Little Lehigh Creek, PA
Monocacy Creek, PA
Mossy Creek, VA
North River, VA
Penns Creek, PA
Spring Creek, PA
Spruce Creek, PA
Valley Creek, PA
Yellow Breeches, PA

TABLE 4: THE LITTLE BLUE-WINGED OLIVE HATCH

Hatch	Scientific Name	Time of Year	Approximate Time to Fish the Dun	Approximate Time to Fish the Spinner	Pattern to Use	Remarks
Little Blue-Winged Olive Dun	*Baetis tricaudatus*	January	1–3 P.M.	3–5 P.M.	Spinner: Rusty Spinner, size 22.	Two broods each year: in March–April, and September–October.
		February	1–3 P.M.	3–5 P.M.	Dun: Blue-Winged Olive Dun, size 20.	
		March	1–3 P.M.	4–5 P.M.		
		April	Noon–5 P.M	4–7 P.M.		
		May	Noon–5 P.M	5–8 P.M.		
	Plauditus veteris and *Baetis tricaudatus*	September	1–6 P.M.	4–7 P.M.	Rusty Spinner, size 20 and 22.	Important late season hatch on limestone streams.
		October	1–4 P.M.	4–7 P.M.	Blue-Winged Olive Dun, size 22.	
		November	1–4 P.M.	4–7 P.M.		
		December	1–3 P.M.	4–7 P.M.		

Sulphur (*Ephemerella rotunda, invaria* and *dorothea*)

The Sulphur is synonymous with limestone waters, and quite often it is the premier hatch of the year on a given limestone stream. And when it appears it often does in tremendous numbers for several weeks. This is the time to catch those lunker limestone trout. On the downside the Sulphur brings hordes of anglers and it's definitely more difficult to fish the hatch in peace and quiet. If you detest crowds then avoid fishing evenings on Spring Creek in central Pennsylvania from mid-May through early June. Go just downstream where Spring Creek enters Bald Eagle Creek. The next five miles of Bald Eagle Creek holds plenty of heavy trout and a few good hatches, and one of them is the Sulphur. The hatch isn't as heavy as the hatch just upstream several miles, but neither is the angling pressure. Here you'll have plenty of room to fish the hatch.

The Green Drake and several other larger species often mask the Sulphur hatch. I have sat and watched Green Drakes and Slate Drakes appear at the same time that the Sulphur did. Invariably the majority of trout feeding do so on the Sulphur. The Sulphur might be a more palatable food than the others. Whatever it is, trout often prefer the smaller Sulphur over the larger Slate and Green Drakes.

Sulphur hatches begin in late April and early May in Virginia and southern Pennsylvania and in mid-May in central Pennsylvania. The first

Trout prefer to eat the Sulphur even when larger food like the Green Drake is on the water.

two or three days they appear they often do so in the afternoon. After that short spurt in the afternoon, the hatch then shifts to the evening, around 8:30 P.M. Sulphur Spinners become important after an evening or two. In fact, spinners often become so important that they compete with duns for the trout's attention. If you plan to fish a limestone stream in May or June make certain that you carry patterns to match the dun and the spinner.

Beaver Creek, MD
Beaver Creek, VA
Big Fishing Creek, PA
Buffalo Run, PA
Cedar Run, PA
Clover Creek, PA
Falling Spring Branch, PA
Honey Creek, PA
Kishacoquillas Creek, PA
Letort Spring Run, PA
Lititz Run, PA
Little Juniata River, PA
Little Lehigh Creek, PA
Lower Bald Eagle, PA
Monocacy Creek, PA
Mossy Creek, VA
North River, VA
Penns Creek, PA
Piney Creek, PA
Saucon Creek, PA
Spring Creek, PA
Tea Creek, PA
Warriors Mark Run, PA
Yellow Breeches, PA

TABLE 5: THE SULPHUR HATCH

Hatch	Scientific Name	Time of Year	Approximate Time to Fish the Dun	Approximate Time to Fish the Spinner	Pattern to Use	Remarks
Sulphur	*Ephemerella rotunda* and *Ephemerella invaria*	May	1–4 P.M. for first two days; then 8:30 P.M.	8:30 P.M.	Sulphur Dun and Spinner, size 16.	Once the hatch begins it usually continues for three weeks or more.
Sulphur	*Ephemerella rotunda,* *Ephemerella invaria,* and *Ephemerella dorothea*	June	8:30 P.M.	8:30 P.M.	Sulphur Dun and Spinner, size 16.	
Sulphur/ Pale Evening Dun	*Ephemerella dorothea*	July	8:45 P.M.	8:45 P.M.	Pale Evening Dun and Spinner, size 18.	

Blue-Winged Olive Dun (*Drunella cornuta, walkeri, cornutella*)

Blue-Winged Olives also frequent many limestone waters. You'll find the nymphs swimming freely streamwide. Several common mayfly species make up the vague grouping of Blue-Winged Olives. Probably the two most common are a size-14 critter (*Drunella cornuta*) that appears in late morning near the end of May and a size-16 mayfly (*Drunella cornutella*) that appears from mid-June through early July.

The smaller Blue-Winged Olive, a size-16, can often be found on limestone streams for more than two or even three weeks. But with normal weather conditions the dun escapes from the water's surface rapidly. That is, unless it meets cool, drizzly, overcast conditions. When this dun escapes rapidly you can expect to see few trout feeding on the surface. If that's the case then fish a nymph or emerger and wait until evening for the spinner fall. The spinner is often the more dependable phase to fish.

For the lazy angler, there's the Blue-Winged Olive, which usually doesn't appear until late morning.

Once the hatch has begun you can expect to fish over trout rising to the spinner fall every evening around 7 or 8 P.M. for a couple weeks. The trout seem to become highly selective with the body color more than with any other spinner fall that I've ever encountered, except the Trico. I mix nine parts of black poly to one part of dark olive to get the olive-black body color of the natural spinner.

If you pursue the large Blue-Winged Olive just right you sometimes see a concentrated hatch around 11 A.M. near the end of May. On some of the smaller limestone streams like the very upper end of Spruce and Spring Creeks—and I am certain many more—you will find occasional Blue-Winged Olives appearing much of the summer.

Big Fishing Creek, PA
Elk Creek, PA
Honey Creek, PA
Little Juniata River, PA

TABLE 6: THE BLUE-WINGED OLIVE DUN HATCH

Hatch	Scientific Name	Time of Year	Approximate Time to Fish the Dun	Approximate Time to Fish the Spinner	Pattern to Use	Remarks
Blue-Winged Olive Dun	*Drunella cornuta*	Late May	11 A.M.– 1 P.M.	8:30 P.M.	Blue-Winged Olive Dun, size 14.	Spinner is often more important to angling than the dun.
	Drunella cornutella	June	Morning and afternoon	7 P.M.	Same, size 16.	
		June	Morning and afternoon	7 P.M.	Same, size 16.	
		July	Morning and afternoon	7 P.M.		

Mossy Creek, VA

Penns Creek, PA

Pine Creek, PA

Spring Creek, PA (upper end)

Spruce Creek, PA

Yellow Breeches, PA

Yellow Creek, PA

Green Drake

(*Ephemera guttulata* and other burrowers like *Hexagenia rigida*)

The first time I fished the Green Drake occurred more than thirty-six years ago. The whole event was a serendipitous mistake. I didn't know anything about the hatch until I arrived on Penns Creek near Coburn at 9 A.M. The minute I arrived I knew something was up. Even that early in the morning, cars filled most of the parking spaces along the stream. Everywhere I looked I saw anglers sitting along the stream. I stopped at the first open space and walked and talked to the nearest angler. He said

You have to wait until dusk for the Green Drake to emerge. The Coffin Fly pattern imitates the Green Drake spinner.

he was just passing the time until the big event that evening. When I asked what that big event was he blurted out that this was the day the Green Drake appears. Moreover, he said the hatch would not occur until dusk. That meant I had twelve hours to fish and wait. I headed to a nearby fly shop and purchased a couple patterns the owner recommended: some Green Drakes to imitate the emerging dun and Coffin Flies to copy the spinners.

I fished only halfheartedly waiting for this supposedly big event to occur in the evening. As I did more and more anglers arrived streamside. All anglers had one thing on their mind: the Green Drake.

Finally the hatch came off. The huge mayflies appeared near dusk and the surface went crazy with trout chasing the big duns. The hatch lasted well past dark and most of the anglers stayed until the last dun had hatched. I caught only two trout on that initial meeting with the Green Drake. But I was hooked for life.

A cousin to the Green Drake is the Dark Green Drake, found on smaller limestone streams.

The Little Juniata River had held a great Green Drake for a decade, but it lost this giant hatch in 1996. Recent reports indicate that this mayfly has returned.

Big Fishing Creek, PA (upper end)
Cove Creek, PA
Elk Creek, PA
Elk Creek, WVA
Honey Creek, PA
Little Juniata River, PA
Mossy Creek, VA
Penns Creek, PA
Spruce Creek, PA (lower half)
Warriors Mark Run, PA
Yellow Creek, PA

Another Drake cousin, the Slate Drake, emerges from the faster stretches of water in limestones.

In June and July, the Yellow Drake hatch appears over slow currents.

TABLE 7: THE GREEN DRAKE HATCH

Hatch	Scientific Name	Time of Year	Approximate Time to Fish the Dun	Approximate Time to Fish the Spinner	Pattern to Use	Remarks
Green Drake	*Ephemera guttulata*	Late May	8 P.M.	8:30 P.M.	Size 8	Size varies from stream to stream.

White Fly (*Ephoron leukon*)

The White Fly appears on eastern, midwestern, and western waters from late July into early September. These mayflies usually appear in late summer just as dusk approaches. Some of the heaviest hatches in the East appear on the Yellow Breeches in southern Pennsylvania. Up to a few years ago the Little Juniata River boasted a respectable hatch of these unusual mayflies. After the January flood in 1996 something happened to the river and many of its hatches. One of the hatches to disappear after that event was the White Fly. But recently the White Fly, like the Green Drake, has begun to reappear on the river.

The White Fly is a member of the ancient genus *Ephoron*. The male changes from dun to spinner within minutes after it emerges, but the female does not transform. The White Fly female dun is one of the very few mayflies that emerges and lays eggs as a dun. On warm late August and early September evenings the dun fall often continues well past dark. If you can find some open water that gets relatively little angling pressure then you can experience some of the greatest fishing of the season.

The Susquehanna River and Juniata River host heavy hatches of this mayfly for more than a month. The hatch appears in the Harrisburg area around the middle of July and works its way up the two rivers. On the Susquehanna near Tunkhannock the hatch appears in early August. In the town of West Pittston authorities often close the steel bridge across the Susquehanna River in early August when these insects appear. Thousands of dead and dying White Flies land on the bridge, making the roads slippery

TABLE 8: THE WHITE FLY HATCH

Hatch	Scientific Name	Time of Year	Approximate Time to Fish the Dun	Approximate Time to Fish the Spinner	Pattern to Use	Remarks
White Fly	*Ephoron leukon*	Mid- to late August	8 P.M.	8:30 P.M.	White Wulff, size 14.	Female dun never changes to a spinner.

and driving extremely dangerous. On the upper end of the Little Juniata the hatch continues sometimes well into September. Look for the hatch on the lower end of many of the limestone streams entering the Juniata and Susquehanna Rivers. If you find cool water and the White Fly hatch then you'll find late-season rising trout.

> Frankstown Branch, Juniata River, PA
> Juniata River, PA (also, the first couple hundred feet of any Juniata limestone tributary that empties into the Susquehanna River)
> Little Juniata River, PA
> Lower Bald Eagle, PA (very spotty)
> Yellow Breeches, PA

5

Tactics for Limestone Streams

To this day I still think about the incident with Vince Marinaro and the Tricos on Falling Spring Branch that I recounted in the introduction. I often wonder how I would have reacted differently to that situation armed with what I know today. Almost fifty years later anglers now have many new implements and tactics to catch trout. First and foremost is the improvement in leaders and tippets. With the advent of fluorocarbons and strong leaders we can now use finer leaders and not worry about losing every fish we hook. Fluorocarbons give us the added advantage of nearly invisible tippets connecting the leader to the fly. These and other developments elevate fly-fishing tactics a notch or two.

So many new tactics have come to us in the past half-century that I'm certain Vince would have tried some of them and readily coped with the situation. He could have changed patterns and substituted one a size or two smaller. That seems to work in many instances on heavily fished waters. He might have changed his tippet and used a fluorocarbon one. I don't think he would have tried sinking the pattern to give trout a different look—that might have gone over the edge for him. We now recognize that trout often feed on sunken Trico spinners long after the hatch has ended, but Vince was committed to a Trico dry fly. I feel certain that he would not have resorted to some of the other tactics that I recommend here.

Anglers have also learned about other ways that they can cope with frustrating hatches and spinner falls, especially on heavily fished limestone waters. Many fly fishers now recognize that if they fish the hatch or spinner fall the first week that the hatch has appeared, then they have a better chance of catching trout. Anglers have also discovered that if they fish the hatches on overcast days the emerging duns rest for a considerably longer period of time before they are ever able to take flight. But many of us don't have the flexibility to take off and fish any time the weather is threatening. That day with Vince fifty years ago was cool but not inclement, and the Trico had already appeared for more than a month when we fished it.

Nothing works continuously and no tactic is foolproof. But the tactics detailed in this chapter just might outwit highly selective trout, especially those on pressured streams.

SPECIAL TACTICS FOR SELECTIVE TROUT

1. Use a long, fine leader with a fluorocarbon tippet.
2. Avoid drag.
3. Sink the spinner or dun pattern if a floating one doesn't work.
4. Use a smaller pattern.
5. Use a pattern that successful local anglers use.
6. Carry several different patterns that match the same hatch.
7. Carry plenty of patterns to match midges and scuds.
8. Fish on lousy days.
9. Look for and fish areas other anglers avoid.
10. Approach the stream carefully.
11. Look for feeding trout.
12. Hire a guide.

USE A LONG, FINE LEADER WITH A FLUOROCARBON TIPPET

Fishing heavily fished waters—limestone or freestone—calls for long, fine leaders. I strongly urge that you use fluorocarbon tippets. Recent advances with increased strength and lower visibility of these tippets will help you even more. We'll look at both the length of the leader, and the type and diameter of the tippet.

Fluorocarbon Leaders

Until a few years ago I thought diameter or the type of leader didn't matter much. I changed my mind completely after a trip to Montana in 1997.

My son, Bryan, Ken Rictor, and Lynn Rotz accompanied me on the trip. Jerry Armstrong was our guide. We spent a day fishing near Alder, Montana, on some small, spring-fed ponds formed more than a century ago by gold-mining operations. These small ponds had an abundant supply of cool spring water entering at different places. Ken, Lynn, and Bryan headed off to other ponds while I remained at the largest in the series, the one closest to the car. In about an hour all three returned looking dejected. In that hour of fishing not one of them had caught a trout or even had a strike. When they asked me how I had done I told them that I landed seven trout. All of us wondered at the big discrepancy. We compared flies, tactics, and leaders and discovered that I used a fluorocarbon tippet while they had tied standard tippets on their leaders, all 6X. That was the only difference we could determine, so I added a 6X fluorocarbon tippet to each of their leaders. Within minutes all three had heavy brown trout on their lines. Within an hour they caught more than ten trout. After that experience with fluorocarbon tippets, we immediately headed for Tom Harmon's Orvis shop in Sheridan, about ten miles away. We bought every pack of 5X and 6X Mirage that he had in his store.

A couple years ago I conducted a series of tests on leaders. You can read more about these experiments in the book, *How to Catch More Trout*. I fished the same 200-foot area of a private limestone stream using regular and fluorocarbon tippets. With each smaller-sized tippet, especially with the fluorocarbon ones, I caught more trout, and in many cases I experienced a significant increase in the number of fish (see Table 9). So tippet diameter, and whether or not the tippet is fluorocarbon, appears to be the key.

In the tests I used a tandem setup with a Patriot dry fly and a size-12 weighted Cream Glo Bug. I fished 10½-foot leaders with 4X, 5X, and 6X regular tippets, and 4X, 5X, and 6X fluorocarbon tippets. I used six fly rods with the different tippets. I wanted to compare the value of regular tippets versus those made of fluorocarbon material. I cast each twenty-five times then switched to the next fly rod. I cast each fly rod a total of a hundred times and recorded the number of trout caught. I conducted the tests in August when the water was extremely low and clear, with a bright sun shining over head. Since I used the same two patterns for all of the experiments it showed how productive the leaders really were. Making a hundred casts is not nearly enough to prove anything *scientifically*, but it still opened my eyes.

TABLE 9: TIPPET TESTS ON LIMESTONE STREAM TROUT

Tippet Size	Diameter of the Tippet Connecting to the Dry Fly and the Wet Fly	Leader Type: Regular (R), Fluoro-carbon (F)	Number of Trout Caught on the Dry Fly in 100 Casts	Number of Trout Caught on the Wet Fly in 100 Casts	Total Number of Trout
4X	.007	R	0	2	2
4X	.007	F	0	4	4
5X	.006	R	0	3	3
5X	.006	F	2	6	8
6X	.005	R	0	4	4
6X	.005	F	4	12	16

What conclusions did I draw from the tests? First, fluorocarbons appear to work. Second, use the finest possible fluorocarbon leader you can. Of course, there's a tradeoff: If you use 6X and 7X you're more likely to break off heavier trout. On clear days with low water start off with 5X or 6X fluorocarbon tippets. You might have to go lighter.

There's another interesting aspect to the experiments. Using the tandem setup I did not catch any trout on the dry fly in that very clear water until I used a 5X fluorocarbon tippet. I caught even more trout on the Patriot dry fly when I used a 6X fluorocarbon. I feel confident that had I used a 7X fluorocarbon leader I would have done even better.

Despite this and other positive tests many anglers still refuse to use fluorocarbons for a number of reasons. They refuse to pay three times as much for fluorocarbon leaders. But I say that if I catch three or four times as many trout with a more expensive leader it's worth the price. And some anglers argue that when they use fluorocarbons they lose some tippet strength. That might have been true until recent innovations. Now some fluorocarbons have become stronger. Rio Fluoroflex Plus, for example, in 4X now has a test of 7 pounds; the older Fluoroflex had a 5-pound test rating. The new Rio 7X fluorocarbon boasts a 2½-pound test strength. Orvis has reformulated its Mirage fluorocarbon, making it much stronger.

Other fly fishers contend that these fluorocarbons sink. Orvis now claims that its New Mirage sinks just beneath the surface and prevents those telltale shadows. Newer fluorocarbons also have reduced visibility. Regular Orvis Super Strong leader has a refractory index of 1.53 percent, which is fairly good. New Mirage has a refractory index of only 0.09 percent, making this leader almost invisible to fish.

The trout's reaction to the patterns used during the test period was interesting. On the 4X and 5X tests trout often came up to the wet or dry fly and turned away. I thought they refused the pattern. When I used the 6X fluorocarbon tippet (to connect the dry fly and the wet fly) those same trout that refused the heavier tippets now took the same flies on a lighter fluorocarbon tippet. Trout hadn't refused the pattern—they rejected the visible leader. Keep that in mind as you fish on those late summer trips even on limestone streams you will often encounter clear skies and low water. If trout seem to refuse your flies then switch to a lighter tippet. On those late summer trips I often start with a 6X fluorocarbon tippet. I might eventually change to a 7X fluorocarbon tippet before trout take the fly, especially trout on heavily fished streams.

Indeed, on more heavily fished limestone streams you might have to resort to a 7X fluorocarbon to catch trout. Recently I fished the Lee's Ferry section of the Colorado River in northern Arizona. This most certainly is not a limestone stream but it is heavily fished tailwater and the outcome here should compare closely to limestone streams. Howard Nixon and Gary Hitterman, both of Casa Grande, Arizona, accompanied me in the boat. Our guide for the day was Dave Trimble, a 24-year-old veteran of the river. I consider Dave one of the top guides that I've fished with over the past twenty years. One thing about Dave: He complained loudly that day that the largest trout he ever caught on the river was an 18-inch rainbow and he was tired of apologizing to his clients because he hadn't caught a larger fish. Dave had few days off and guided clients almost every day, so he had scarce time to fly fish.

Howard, Gary, and I fished for the first four hours and we caught plenty of rainbows. I then walked over to Dave, handed him my fly rod, and told him we were going to catch a larger trout for him today so he would no longer have to apologize to his clients. I became the guide and Dave became the client.

We first tied on a tandem with a Patriot dry fly and a Blueberry wet fly. The Blueberry is nothing more than a Bead Head Glo Bug dyed with Rit evening-blue dye and tied with six turns of .010 lead that I shove up under the bead. I handed Dave a 3-foot piece of 7X fluorocarbon to connect the dry fly and the wet fly. Why 7X? The section of the river we fished saw a half dozen fly fishers each day of the week. I then cautioned Dave that we should use a stronger knot, especially on the 2-pound test 7X fluorocarbon tippet. We chose the Duncan Loop, rather than an improved clinch knot to connect the leader to the flies, because in tests (see Table 10) the loop was much stronger.

Dave began casting in backwater that held some larger trout. On his fourth cast a trout struck the wet fly. I knew immediately it was one of Lee's Ferry's behemoths. The trout headed downstream and Dave followed. Finally, a half hour later, Dave netted the 24-inch beauty. Dave had done everything just right and was handsomely rewarded for his efforts. Finally he could brag, and rightly so. Fluorocarbons work.

Recently, complete fluorocarbon leaders have come onto the market. I think this is overkill. You don't need an entire leader made of fluorocarbon. I can just tie on a fluorocarbon tippet to a leader made up of regular, less expensive leader.

Knots

With finer leaders, knot strength becomes even more important. A recent study of knot strength (see Table 10) by the Rio Line Company reveals some interesting results. The best knot for connecting tippet to fly in the test was the Duncan Loop. The worst knot is the widely used improved clinch knot. It's not uncommon on limestone streams to tie on a 7X fluorocarbon tippet with 2-pound test strength. So would you rather connect that leader to the fly with a clinch knot, an improved clinch knot, or a Duncan Loop?

Leader Length

Leader length is critical for several reasons. First, the longer the leader often the better drift you get with the fly. And in most cases you want to avoid drag (see below). But leader length can also be important when you cast smaller flies—with a longer leader you often get more finesse with the fly landing on the surface. I like knotted leaders, but sometimes they become a handicap on limestone waters with plenty of weeds and algae. Despite that I do believe they consistently cast more accurately than a knotless one.

On some of the less pressured limestone streams I start with a 10½-foot leader with a 5X fluorocarbon tippet. You often have to go even finer on some heavily fished urban limestone streams. Al Miller and Rich

TABLE 10: RIO LINE COMPANY KNOT-STRENGTH
TEST RESULTS

Connection	Type of Knot	Percent of Strength	Rank
Leader to Leader: Fluoroflex 4X to Powerflex 3X (5-pound to 8.2-pound)	Triple surgeon	88	1
	Four-turn water knot (tied wet)	85	2
	Four-turn water knot (dry)	81	3
	Five-turn blood knot	81	4
	Double surgeon	73	5
Leader to Fly: Knot test (6.4-pound test Powerflex)	Ducan Loop	94	1
	Uni knot	93	2
	Clinch*	92	3
	Lefty Loop	83	5
	Turle	82	6
	Improved clinch	78	7

* The clinch knot slipped many times in the tests. These were not taken into account.

Heiserman will tell you that if you want any modicum of success on the Little Lehigh you've got to start out with a 12- to 15-foot leader and a 6X or 7X tippet. Al and Rich are possibly the two top fly fishers on that heavily fished stream, and they understand the need for a finer, longer tippet there.

Don't even attempt to fish the Little Lehigh or many other limestone waters like Mossy Creek in Virginia, or Yellow Creek in southwestern Pennsylvania, during a Trico hatch with anything less than a 10-foot leader. Shorter leaders scare pressured trout and also promote drag.

AVOID DRAG

I try to spend one day a week experimenting. On that day I often test new patterns, different techniques, and new equipment. I've tested some wild ideas, some that never helped me one bit.

I spent one recent summer morning watching some angling friends cast to trout in the same pool and riffle section of a limestone creek. I had fished this section frequently over the past year so I knew it held quite a few trout.

All of these fly fishers used the same pattern, a Dark Olive Bead Head Caddis trailing behind a size-12 Patriot dry fly. I consider these anglers fairly skilled fly fishers. In that section one angler caught a half dozen trout, another caught one, and the third angler caught no trout. The person who caught the six trout was not the first to fish that section of the stream, but the last.

From my excellent vantage point I watched all of them cast the fly, and then I followed the drift through the riffle and pool below. After a half day of watching I became more convinced than ever that there was one thing that generated success or failure that day on that stream: drag. The two anglers who caught the fewest number of trout in the experiment had the most drag.

Drag is the uneven or unnatural drift of the fly with current: The fly floats either slower or faster than the stream flow and thus looks entirely fake. "Micro drag" is the almost imperceptible slower or faster movement of the dry or wet fly.

Drag is easy enough to see, but how can you detect micro drag? I often follow a leaf, bubble, or other free-floating object on the surface close to my fly. When a hatch is on I follow the imitation with the drift of naturals. By watching an object floating freely near your fly, you can easily detect whether your fly has the least bit of drag or not.

What about an area where you have water flowing at three or four different speeds? Here is where drag occurs very quickly. How many times have you seen trout feed in these areas of multiple currents? They seem to select these because they can readily tell an imitation from a real insect floating drag free.

There are several ways to prevent micro drag: a slack leader cast; a longer, finer tippet; mending your line; changing your location and fishing downstream. All will help. But slack leader cast is one of the most important things you can do to prevent drag. Yet few anglers are skilled at it.

George Harvey, progenitor of the slack-leader cast, demonstrates the technique on a limestone near his home in Pennsylvania.

Pennsylvania limestone veteran George Harvey has preached the slack-leader cast technique for years. Aim the dry fly about three feet above the surface and stop the forward cast short. Then bring the fly rod down by your side. By quickly moving the fly rod down by your side you make curves in the leader, rather than letting it straighten out. The more curves, the longer the drag-free float. Remember that you want the curves in the leader, but not in your fly line.

Another way to help prevent drag is to mend your line. If you have two currents—a slower one on the far shore and a faster one on the near shore—then mend the line upstream by lifting the rod and making an arc in the fly line. If the current is faster near the far shore than it is near you, then make the arc downstream. As the fly floats downstream I'm constantly making small mends—maybe ten to twenty of them. Too many anglers I've watched make one large mend when the fly first settles on the surface. That big mend often yanks the dry fly out of the water and scares

The results of a drag-free drift: a fine brown trout taken by Mr. Harvey himself.

any trout nearby. Be careful because if you make too exaggerated a mend at the beginning of a drift it will also take all the slack S-curves out of your leader.

A third way you can prevent micro drag is to attach a longer, finer tippet. A finer and longer tippet will make more S-curves and allow for a longer drag-free drift. If you're using a 2-foot tippet, increase it by a half-foot or more.

All things being equal, the longer you have that correct fly pattern on the water, with a long, fine leader, and floating drag free, the more trout you'll catch. Yet, I often see anglers who are constantly casting and only occasionally drop the fly on the water. I sometimes get the feeling that they're enthralled with their casting ability. Why do they do this? One word: drag. They see that the pattern isn't drifting with the current so they cast and try again. Keep that fly on or in the surface as long as possible *without drag.*

I said earlier that multiple currents really present a problem with drag and especially micro drag. There are sections of some of my favorite streams that I often avoid because it's almost impossible to get a drag-free float. But these areas often hold trout because they seldom get fished properly.

Remember the saying that some fly fishers use to wish each other success? They say, "Tight lines." That brings up the subject of drag versus setting the hook. There's a fine line between tempting drag and the ability to set the hook quickly on a strike. If you have no bends or curves in your leader or line it's easy to set the hook. But, too tight a line causes drag. Conversely, with too much slack line you can't set the hook properly. Remember how much line your fly rod can take up when you lift it for a strike and fish accordingly. You can test it with your fly rod when you begin fishing. That's why I prefer using a 9-foot fly rod on most occasions. Shorter rods don't give you the luxury of being able to throw as much slack line as you might need to prevent drag, or being able to quickly lift a lot of line for a quick strike.

SINK THE DUN OR SPINNER PATTERN

Over thirty years ago I experienced frustration with the Trico hatch and spinner fall on the Falling Spring Branch. This occurred a few years after fishing the hatch with Barry Beck and Vince Marinaro. But like Vince, I too became frustrated one morning during the height of the Trico spinner fall. Trout rose all around me but I couldn't nab one. Finally I hooked and landed a small rainbow that was nothing to brag about. Upstream about thirty feet, an old angler on the opposite bank released his seventh trout while I released my first. Soon he caught another, then another, while I just watched him land all of those rainbows.

What was he doing differently? Was it his pattern? Maybe he used a longer, finer leader. I blurted out, "What the devil are you doing to catch all of those trout?"

The old codger paused for a second or two in his casting rhythm, looked towards me, and didn't say a word. After about ten minutes he wound in his line, looked back at me, and in a voice I could barely hear he said, "I'm sinking the fly."

Wow. Why did he sink the fly? I left the stream myself a few minutes later and headed for the Mont Alto Campus of Penn State University. I had a meeting scheduled there. On the way to the campus, during the meeting, and on my trip back to my home, I kept hearing those words: *I'm sinking the fly*. Then I thought about all of those Trico spinners that fell spent on the surface upstream a mile or two. What happens to them on their drift downstream? The stream held plenty of rapids. Would these dead and dying spinners sink underneath the surface, especially after floating through a series of riffles? Wouldn't some of the trout that had been fished over for several months with this hatch seek out these easier-to-reach spinners under the surface? Suddenly I realized that old codger had sunk his Trico spinner and caught all those trout on a "wet fly."

I couldn't wait to get to my fly tying desk. I tied up a dozen spinner patterns that were made of materials that would readily sink and also had a few wraps of 0.005 lead wound around the shank.

I first tried the sinking Trico pattern on the Ruby River in Montana and it worked there. But would it work on the Little Lehigh?

The Little Lehigh near Allentown, Pennsylvania, probably holds more anglers on a per day basis than any other stream in the East. I often conducted fly-fishing workshops there for Rod Rohrbach who operates the Little Lehigh Fly Shop located within forty feet of this fertile limestone creek. Rod asked me to conduct a class in late July more than a decade ago. The class was to begin at noon and run until 5 P.M. The title of the class was, "How to Catch More Trout." I arrived several hours early to fish the often frustrating Trico hatch. I wanted to relay to the class how easy it was even to catch trout on a heavily fished stream during a hatch if you used the proper tactics.

The spinner fall became heavy around 8:30 A.M. on that cloudy, cool late July morning. Trout fed heavily on the spinners just a hundred yards downstream from the fly shop. Soon several other anglers joined me and cast over trout feeding on the spent spinners. We cast and cast and cast without even bringing one trout to the surface. I used a 12-foot leader with a 6X fluorocarbon tippet and a size-24 Trico spinner imitation to no avail. All of us complained that these trout had been fished over for more than a month with dozens of patterns to match the spinner fall. To make matters worse, I soon found out that two of the anglers nearby were registered to take my class that afternoon.

Increasing anxiety jolted loose my memory of the same situation that had confronted me several years before on the Ruby River in Montana. I pulled out from my vest that secret box of weighted Trico spinners. After three years of no use, the flies still looked good. I tied one on about 18 inches behind a size-16 Patriot dry fly in a tandem rig.

I carefully watched the white-winged Patriot and if that sank or hesitated I was prepared to set the hook quickly. Maybe I made a dozen casts and drifts with the rig before the dry fly sank. I set the hook and took a decent Little Lehigh brown trout on the sunken spinner. In a few more casts I had another trout on the line. I landed five trout that morning on that sunken spinner pattern—right in front of those other fellows. I felt much better about teaching that class.

So if you don't catch trout on the dry fly you are using and don't have weighted flies, twitch the fly underneath the surface and fish it there. That same tactic has saved me from many barren fishing trips on limestone streams.

Sinking the pattern not only works when a spinner fall occurs, but also when duns appear. This works for the Green Drake. On Penns Creek one evening I hadn't caught a trout and the drake hatch had already appeared for more than an hour. Finally, in a desperate move, I began twitching my large Green Drake dry fly so it drifted a few inches under the surface. On the very next cast I hooked a 19-inch brown trout. I continued that technique for the next hour and landed two more trout.

Remember, if you have matched a hatch and trout aren't taking your fly then sink that pattern—be it a spinner or dun—and fish it underneath. With the dun pattern impart some motion to the fly to suggest emergence. With a spinner pattern fish it on a dead drift.

USE A SMALLER PATTERN

On any heavily pressured stream, using small flies is very important. Dick Henry, one of the premier fly fishers in Pennsylvania, has fished and written about limestone waters like the Tulpehocken and Quittapahilla Creeks in southeastern Pennsylvania for more than a half century. I consider him one of the top authorities on limestone fishing. In a recent letter to me, Dick spelled out his beliefs on pattern selection and angling pressure:

> Trout that are under heavy fishing pressure are almost impossible to catch. Despite a few good days fishing the Trico on the Tulpe-hocken, frustrating times were more common. I remember when netting fifteen to twenty trout [during the hatch] was very common, but no more. Typically if they come easy, it occurs early in

the rise [at the beginning of the spinner fall]. After that they look and turn away, or they appear to take the fly but they don't get hooked. Ten years ago I took trout easily on a size-22 imitation, but now I'm using a size-26 pattern and feeling that perhaps the flies aren't small enough.

I believe Mark Fortuna has the right idea [when it comes to matching the Trico spinner]. Tie a size-28 fly on a size-26 hook, open the hook slightly and bend the point either to the right or left—and set the hook quickly when a fish takes your fly. Mark believes that a fish can eject a fly quickly enough to avoid being hooked if the angler's response is even slightly delayed.

Those are true words of wisdom. If you encounter a heavily fished stream and you are fishing over a hatch or spinner fall that has appeared daily for the past several weeks then it is imperative that you follow his advice. Use a smaller pattern with a finer leader and watch that fly very closely so that you are ready to strike immediately.

Bob Toolan recommends that you use small flies in late summer on Allentown limestone streams: size-18 or smaller Bead Head Pheasant Tails, Hare's Ear, and scuds. These small patterns work well on those hot, low-water conditions.

USE PATTERNS THAT SUCCESSFUL LOCAL ANGLERS USE

Recall Al's Rat. It continues to work on the Little Lehigh year after year. Most major limestone streams have special patterns that seem to be especially effective on them. If you are new to a famous limestone stream, stop in one of the local fly shops or talk to some of the regulars and ask them what they use to catch trout.

I'll never forget that story George Harvey tells about a fly he developed called the Harvey Special. As a freshman in college in the early 1930s, George asked the dean of the College of Agriculture if he could fish with him on opening day on Spring Creek. The dean took George with him, dropped him off two miles upstream, and told him to fish downstream where he'd be waiting for him. While George fished his way downstream he hit an opening-day Grannom caddisfly hatch. George had tied a fly that matched this hatch perfectly and he called it the Harvey Special: a simple caddis fly with a black body. When George finally met up with the dean downstream he showed him his catch—25 huge trout (this was in the days when everybody kept every fish). The dean had caught only two small trout. Do specialized patterns work well on limestone streams? You bet. To this day the Harvey Special still takes its share.

CARRY SEVERAL DIFFERENT PATTERNS THAT MATCH THE SAME HATCH

On some of the more common hatches I carry three and four different patterns that match the same hatch. For the Sulphur hatch I carry a standard high-riding Sulphur pattern, one tied parachute style, and a Comparadun type. If you only have a high-riding dry fly and the trout refuse it, try cutting off the hackle on the underside so it rides more flush with the surface. I always carry one Sulphur pattern that matches both the dun *and* the spinner, because I can't even tell you the number of times I tied a Sulphur dun on my tippet only to witness a great Sulphur spinner fall in the evening.

Don't ever depend on just one pattern. I'm convinced that one of the problems with the Trico spinner fall is that just about everybody uses identical patterns. Over the many weeks that the hatch appears the trout tend to reject that pattern more and more.

Do the same with the Green Drake hatch: carry at least two different patterns and if one doesn't work, switch to the other.

So, there are two tactical fly changes that you've got to remember on limestone streams. First, when trout reject a fly, try the same pattern a size smaller. Second, if the smaller pattern doesn't work, switch to a different pattern that matches the same hatch.

CARRY PLENTY OF PATTERNS TO MATCH MIDGES AND SCUDS

A lot of action occurs on limestone streams out of sight of the angler. Trout have the normal array of mayfly and stonefly nymphs. They also can feed on emerging caddis pupa and free-swimming caddis, and cranefly and midge larvae. But what we often forget is that trout feed all day long on the very common freshwater shrimp that we call scud. I've often watched trout slowly examine every aquatic weed in search of these morsels. I learned this lesson the hard way from an old limestone fly fisher more than forty years ago.

"Young man, it's too early to be using that dry fly," the old fellow said to me on the Fisherman's Paradise section of Spring Creek.

"What do you mean?" I said.

"The trout aren't looking up yet," he replied.

Note the numerous flies on this angler's vest—he used a host of flies matching the same hatch until he nabbed this Spruce Creek brown.

He explained that the trout had been accustomed to feeding on or near the bottom for five months and they haven't seen much food on the surface. Thus, they weren't looking up.

That made sense, and I've heard a few more old timers say the same thing. But until two decades ago I seldom used a wet fly or fished midge and scud patterns. I carried a few small dry flies like the Griffith's Gnat in sizes 22 to 26 to match an occasional midge, but that was it. So, even after that conversation with the wise old angler I continued to cast that gray-bodied Adams dry fly time and time again on that late March day without even one strike.

I quit fishing for a few minutes and walked over to the old angler and asked him what he used on winter and early spring days. He showed me a small wet fly that looked like a precursor to the now common Zebra Midge. It copied a midge pupa. I watched the old codger fish that thing for more than a half hour. Why not? I hadn't done a thing on this heavily fished water. He caught two trout and missed a couple others on that pattern. Finally he turned around and handed me one of these flies and told me to try it. I hadn't really fished a wet fly since I graduated from high school and began using dries. I did, however, catch two trout on that wet fly that morning.

A Zebra Midge in sizes 16 to 20 in several colors will work all year round in most limestone waters. On the rare occasion when the Zebra Midge doesn't work then I fall back on a size-16 to size-20 Brassie or a Scud pattern like the Simple Shrimp. I feel confident that one of those three patterns will catch trout most of the year on limestone streams that harbor good midge hatches and *gammarus* species.

What happens if you see no activity at all on the limestone stream you plan to fly fish? If you see any aquatic weeds inspect them to see if the stream holds scuds or other aquatic life. On one of the first days I fished Spruce Creek I fished a wet fly and thought I had a strike. Instead I brought in a bunch of roots. When I tried to disconnect my fly from the tangled, gnarled mess of roots I noticed hundreds of free-swimming green caddis larvae moving around on the roots. I tied on a size-14 Olive Caddis larva pattern and caught more than twenty trout that day on that fly. That fly has since become one of my top choices when I'm fishing limestone waters.

Be prepared and always carry some of these patterns with you—and always remember that much happens on a limestone stream out of the sight of the angler. Even if you don't see any activity on the surface that does not mean that trout aren't feeding. There is plenty under the surface and out of view of the angler on which trout can feed. You'll find patterns for all of these types of food in chapter 6.

FISH ON LOUSY DAYS

By far, the most memorable fishing trips I have ever experienced in my fifty years of fly fishing have occurred on lousy, overcast days when a hatch appears. All of these days have occurred on limestone and spring-fed waters. As I said before, I often call the Little Blue-Winged Olive hatch "the lousy day hatch." In *Great Rivers—Great Hatches* I had an entire chapter called "Great Hatches on Lousy Days." Fishing on those days when the sky is overcast, a slight drizzle falls, and the air temperature never rises above the low 60s is always a good move.

When hatching insects appear on the surface and are greeted with cool air temperatures and a drizzle, they are unable to take flight quickly and rest for an extended period on the surface. Trout seize the opportunity. Limestone streams especially display this situation mainly for two reasons. First they often hold more insects than freestones, especially Little Blue-Winged Olives, and, second, their waters are often a bit warmer on those colder days. But there are other great hatches that can appear on those overcast, drizzly days that you encounter throughout the fishing season, as I have encountered on Elk and Penns Creeks, and the Metolius River in Oregon.

Probably one of the greatest and longest lasting hatches was the day my son, Bryan, Vince Gigliotti, and I fished when a Sulphur hatch appeared

This was a cold rainy June day when Bryan Meck, the author's son, nabbed a bunch of wild brown trout on leafy Green Spring.

on Elk Creek in central Pennsylvania. We arrived streamside at 10 A.M. in mid-May and already Sulphurs emerged and trout rose. The hatch continued to appear well into the afternoon and trout fed in every pocket, pool, and riffle. The three of us that day caught more than fifty trout on that extended hatch. A fine drizzle fell the entire time we fished.

LOOK FOR AND FISH AREAS OTHER ANGLERS AVOID

What sets off the real pro from the ordinary angler? The skill to fly fish those areas other anglers are incapable of reaching. You probably know the type of environment I'm talking about: that small, deep, hidden pool just behind a low-hanging hemlock branch; that undercut bank just behind that huge protruding boulder; or that deep run just behind a huge log. The vast majority of anglers avoid making these difficult casts, but able anglers approach these situations as a challenge, and when they do, they catch trout.

Kurt Thomas of Ridgeway, Pennsylvania, is one of those very highly skilled anglers who take these challenges in hand. Kurt guides hundreds of clients on Pennsylvania limestone streams like Spring, Penns, and Big Fishing Creeks. He has done this for the past decade. He is one of the finest casters I have ever seen. What sets Kurt apart from other accomplished fly fishers on these waters? Kurt often looks for those hard-to-fish areas on heavily fished limestone waters. Watch him cast under that low-lying tree or use a "high-stick" approach to guide a nymph far back behind some branches and you'll probably see him catch one, two, or three trout. He'll pick up another one or two trout behind that log that other anglers avoid. Sure, on occasion he'll get hooked to that tree or get caught on that log, but he makes up for those momentary inconveniences by catching plenty of trout even on difficult limestone waters.

The well-known and outstanding fly-fishing writer Buss Grove first gave me this philosophy on fishing these waters. Buss wrote the *Lure and Lore of Trout Fishing* back in the 1950s. When I first fished with Buss on the Little Juniata River I saw him head for some really difficult water near the far shore. He cast that dry fly perfectly under a low-lying tree, and he

Using a high-stick approach this angler probes a shadow under overhanging branches, a tight spot lesser-skilled anglers often pass up.

picked up three trout before I caught one. Buss said that on a heavily fished stream like the Little Juniata River he purposely searches out those hard-to-fish areas because most anglers avoid them.

APPROACH THE STREAM CAREFULLY

Plenty of the limestone streams I talk about here hold good numbers of wild brown trout. A few hold some wild brook trout and some even boast a few wild rainbows. I find many of these wild trout on small streams, those 10 to 15 feet wide. These wild trout didn't grow to be 6, 8, or 10 inches long just by chance—they are truly wild fish. They are trout that dart up- or downstream into a deep pool or under a washed-out bank at any sign of danger.

Many of us have grown up fishing for stocked trout. These hatchery raised trout often don't react the same way wild trout do. Hatchery raised trout have become acclimated to easy food and human activity.

So if you chose a stream that holds wild trout, your approach has to be less conspicuous. Sneak, creep, or crawl or do whatever you have to do to present as low a profile as possible. To achieve any success with the wild brown trout on the Waikaia River, on the South Island in New Zealand, I had to crawl fifty feet to the river's edge. If I didn't, I spooked every trout in the vicinity.

Does clothing matter? You bet. Use drab or neutral colors as much as possible. Earthy colors like olive, brown, or gray work fine.

Remember your shadow, too. Adjust your approach so you have the sun at your back so you're not brightly lit, but don't cast a shadow on the pool or riffle you plan to fish.

LOOK FOR FEEDING TROUT

It seems so obvious, yet few of us do it. If a trout is already feeding it is often easier to catch that fish than one not feeding. When I followed Mike Heck, an Orvis-endorsed guide, on Big Spring recently he searched only for feeding trout. These weren't trout feeding on a hatch of any sort. They fed on scuds and cress bugs. But if you watched them carefully in the clear waters of Big Spring you could easily see them feeding.

That's only part of the solution. Mike feels it is extremely important to drift your pattern directly in front of the fish. To get the pattern directly in front of the feeding fish and deep, Mike uses a lead split-shot. However, the clunking noise of a lead shot landing on the surface tends to scare wary trout, so Mike casts a few feet off to the far side of the fish and then moves the weighted line towards the feeding trout. It's important that the pattern in the final two feet drift naturally—and directly in front of the feeding trout. Bob Toolan, who is an accomplished guide (see Saucon Creek in chapter 2) on southeastern Pennsylvania streams, calls this tactic the "up and over." He often uses this technique and he teaches all of his clients to do the same. It is essential on limestone streams if you want to get food in front of trout feeding below the surface.

HIRE A GUIDE

Are you unfamiliar with the water you plan to fish? Are you relatively new to fly fishing? Do you have just a short time to fly fish? If you have answered yes to any of those questions then you might think about hiring a guide. Back in 1992 when I prepared the manuscript for *Great Rivers— Great Hatches* I fished more than fifty lakes and rivers across the country. To accomplish what I had to know about these waters in a short time I hired guides. That summer I hired and fished with more than forty guides in all, yet I learned more that summer about fly fishing than any other time in my life. I learned the high-stick nymphing technique, fishing the tandem, and much more from these skilled fly fishers.

If you are relative newcomer to the sport then it is imperative that you hire a guide. They can teach you a lot about casting, drag-free drifts, and leader construction. They can show you where to fish. They can cut out a lot of the frustration you normally go through in your formative fly-fishing years.

Back in 1988 when I was writing *Trout Streams and Hatches of Pennsylvania* I found few guides in the Northeast. Now there are hundreds of guides, and many of them specialize on fishing limestone streams. In

Finding a good guide is not hard; check with reputable local fly shops or look up local or regional guide associations to see who is registered.

preparing this book I fished with a few of these guides and I have found them extremely knowledgeable about the hatches, the streams and special techniques needed. Mike Heck, of Chambersburg, Pennsylvania, specializes in guiding on south-central Pennsylvania limestone streams. Kurt Thomas guides on Spring Creek and Big Fishing Creek in central Pennsylvania. There are many other good guides in central Pennsylvania, like Eric Stroup and Skip Galbraith at the Spruce Creek Fly Shop.

If you plan to fly fish southeastern streams then fish with Bob Toolan. On Falling Spring, I consider Mark Sturtevant an extremely capable guide. In Virginia, Brian and Colby Trow and Billy Kingsley will show you some fantastic fishing. These guides and dozens of others in Pennsylvania and Virginia can help you enjoy fly fishing much more. These then are just a few simple rules that will help you on limestone streams, especially those with a wild trout population.

Nothing works consistently and no tactic is fool proof. But you have got to try different tactics and different approaches to fishing limestone streams. I have seen many old-time anglers who won't change their ways. For years and years a plain, old dry fly worked for them and that's what they continue to use with less and less success. While they continue to be set in their ways, other anglers are using finer fluorocarbon tippets, longer leaders, and smaller patterns. If you want to continue to catch trout on limestone streams then you need to be open to new ideas.

6

Tying Patterns for Limestone Hatches

If you want to fly fish for trout, you've got to get buggy. True, you can catch trout on streamers and leech patterns (some big trout, too), but capitalizing on insect activity is the heart of the matter. The terms *nymph, emerger, dun,* and *spinner* are the fly fisherman's bywords. The mayfly, caddisfly, and stonefly are friends, as are the terrestrials, the hoppers and beetles. We constantly compare the flies we tie to these "naturals."

There are, however, some flies that copy no insect and instead contain bright colors designed to irritate trout into striking. Anglers call these patterns "attractors." Patterns like the Patriot and Trout Fin fit into this category, and I talk about them a bit here. I often use a bright attractor type pattern as the lead fly in a tandem rig because it shows up well in any fishing situation, while fishing a "natural" pattern beneath—a nymph or other wet fly.

Let's take a quick look at the four stages of a mayfly and its relation to its imitation, and then I'll supply you with a pretty thorough list of essential fly pattern recipes.

NYMPH PATTERNS

Mayfly nymphs hatch from the fertilized eggs in a couple of weeks to as long as several months later. A nymph spends approximately a year (there are many exceptions) in slow, medium, or fast stretches on rocky or muddy bottoms. Many species are specific to their habitat. After almost a year of growing and shedding its outer covering many times (in growth stages called *instars*), the nymph is ready to emerge.

I'm amazed that most anglers use only one size to copy a particular nymph. The size they most often use is the size of the nymph when it hatches. But let's say you want to use a Light Cahill in April. It would be considerably smaller in size than when it emerges a month or two later. A size-16 pattern might be used to copy the nymph in April. Remember to tie some of the nymphs in sizes smaller than suggested in most recipes. As the nymph lives and feeds for almost a year underwater it is naturally a source of food for feeding fish. Since the nymph is the longest phase of the life cycle, trout have an opportunity to feed on this stage more often than any other stage. Imitations of nymphs work well most of the year because trout feed on this stage almost daily.

Some fly tiers add Sparkle Yarn and Krystal Flash to their nymphal imitations as part of the wing pad. You'll see a recipe for the Flashback Nymph included in this chapter. There's no question that this sparkle or flash brings trout to the pattern, even if it seems a bit unnatural.

EMERGER PATTERNS

After about a year of development the nymph moves toward the surface (many do this near the bottom). Here it sheds its nymphal skin dorsally and becomes a dun. Skilled anglers realize that trout forage on emerging nymphs, and imitate that stage with an emerger that is a hybrid between the nymph and the dun. Often the nymph works well just as the hatch begins. The emerger works well throughout.

How many times have I been frustrated with a hatch? Many times what I thought were rises to hatches were in reality trout feeding on the emergers. The two largest trout I have caught on imitations in the United States both happened when I sank a Green Drake dry fly and fished this floating pattern just a few inches under the surface. What does this tell you? Trout often feed on nymphs that are in the process of transforming into duns. Don't overlook this important phase of fly fishing. And don't forget to add a nymphal shuck to some of your patterns copying the dun. The change from nymph to dun is a gradual one. While the mayfly is shedding its nymphal shuck it is at its most vulnerable stage. Trout sense this and often eat this stage of the emerger readily. Adding a shuck to your pattern copying the nymph can often prove to be the deciding feature whether or not a trout will take a pattern.

Nymphs change to air-breathing mayfly duns in a series of deliberate steps. Most species move towards the surface and rest or ride in surface film for a time; there, the nymph splits open its external skin across its back. Slowly the dun pokes itself out of what was the outer skin of the nymph. First the wings appear, and then the rest of the dun extracts itself out of its old skin. While this whole process is evolving the nymph, emerger, and dun are vulnerable to the trout.

DUN PATTERNS

Many duns ride the surface for some distance before taking flight. Mayflies that appear early or late in the season and those that emerge under poor weather conditions tend to spend more time on the surface before taking flight. These duns are especially important to imitate with dry fly patterns. Patterns like the Hendrickson, Green Drake, and many others have gained notoriety because they match insects that normally take off slowly from the surface. As I said before, trout sense that the most vulnerable part of this entire process of changing from a nymph to a dun is when the nymph is near the surface and in the process of ridding itself of its shuck.

When the dun finally becomes airborne, it usually heads for a nearby tree or bush close to the stream. Duns emerging early in the season sometimes rest on sun-warmed rocks or debris next to the water to protect themselves from early-season freezes.

Although a few mayflies change from a dun to spinner in an hour or less, and a few never change, in most species the transformation requires one or two days. With a final molt, the dun loses its outer covering and reappears over the water as a more brightly colored mayfly with clear glassy wings—the spinner. Spinners meet and mate to complete the life cycle.

SPINNER PATTERNS

The female mayfly spinner, or mature adult (scientists call the spinner an *imago*), mates with the male spinner, usually over fast stretches of a stream and most often in the evening. The male appears over the stream first, waiting for the female spinner. The female, after mating, deposits her fertilized eggs into the water. Some imitations copy the egg sac found on mayfly spinners and caddisflies. The Beaverkill dry fly represents the female Hendrickson spinner with an egg sac. I'm convinced that during a Sulphur spinner fall an angler could catch trout if he or she used a pattern copying just the small yellow egg sac of the mayfly. Try it sometime. Often Grannom down-wing patterns have a turn or two of peacock wound at the rear to imitate the dark olive egg sac of this early season caddisfly.

After the egg laying is completed, many females fall onto the water, usually with wings spent (flat on the surface). When female spinners fall in great numbers on the surface it is both a blessing and a curse to many anglers. Often furious surface feeding occurs at this time. Moreover, this feeding frenzy often happens around dusk and you have to fumble in the half light to tie on a new pattern.

Most spinner imitations copy the spent-winged variety. These patterns usually contain a tail, body, and spent wings of made of poly yarn. Such spent-wing patterns float flush with the surface and are often difficult to locate. I often tie smaller spent spinners like the Trico behind a bright, easy-to-see dry fly on the tandem rig. Don't forget the tactic we discussed in chapter 5: Sink that pattern if trout refuse it on the surface.

It's important to include imitations of some species with divided, upright poly yarn wings. Some Sulphur species, for example, lay their egg sac and remain on the surface with wings upright. Copies of spinners with these upright wings are much easier to locate on the surface at dusk.

With this abbreviated look at the mayfly life cycle you can readily see that all phases of the insect become important sources of food. While the larva of aquatic insects is available every day of the year to trout, adults become available from March through November.

PATTERNS FOR MATCHING LIMESTONE HATCHES

The following collection of recipes details about all the fly patterns you need for fishing both limestone and freestone waters. The wonderful thing about tying flies is that you can customize each one based upon your own observations and in that way develop completely new patterns. Inventing a new fly and having it accepted in the pantheon of patterns is every tier's dream.

Just about all of these patterns call for materials that are well known and easy to get. But you do need a bit of skill to tie some of the smaller patterns. Don't give up, because nothing beats the satisfaction of taking a really nice trout on a fly you tied yourself.

Blue Quill (copies all members of the genus *Paraleptophlebia*)
Thread: Dark gray
Tail: Medium to dark gray hackle fibers
Body: Eyed peacock herl, stripped, or dark gray poly, dubbed.
Wings: Dark gray hackle tips
Hackle: Light to medium blue dun
Shuck (optional): Dark brownish-black Z-lon
Hook: Sizes 18 and 20

You'll need your Blue Quill patterns all through the season, from April to October.

Blue-Quill Nymph
Thread: Dark brown
Tail: Mallard flank feather, dyed dark brown.
Body: Dark brown angora, dubbed.
Wings: One dark gray mallard quill, tied down.
Hackle: Dark gray
Hook: Sizes 16 and 18

Dark Brown Spinner (Blue-Quill species)
Thread: Dark brown
Tail: Dark brown hackle fibers
Body: Dark brown poly, dubbed.
Wings: Pale gray poly yarn, tied spent.
Hook: Sizes 18 and 20

Blue-Winged Olive Dun (copies many species)
Thread: Olive
Tail: Grayish olive hackle fibers
Body: Light to medium olive poly, dubbed.
Wings: Dark gray hackle tips
Hackle: Medium creamish olive
Shuck (optional): Dark olive-black Z-lon
Hook: Sizes 14–20

Blue-Winged Olive Nymph
Thread: Olive
Tail: Wood duck
Body: Dark brown angora tied over, dubbed in olive opossum.
Wings: Brown turkey
Hackle: Ginger variant, dyed olive.
Hook: Sizes 14–18

Blue-Winged Olive patterns imitate many different species; you'll have to match the hatch in color and size carefully.

Dark Olive Spinner (Blue-Winged species)
Thread: Dark olive or black
Tail: Moose mane (dark brown)
Body: Dark olive poly (almost black with an olive cast)
Wings: Pale gray poly yarn, tied spent.
Hook: Sizes 14–20

Brown Drake (copies *Ephemera simulans*)
Thread: Dark brown
Tail: Moose mane
Body: Yellowish brown poly, dubbed.
Wings: Mallard flank feather, dyed yellowish brown, divided.
Hackle: Rear, cream; front, dark brown
Shuck (optional):Tannish-gray Z-lon
Hook: Sizes 10 and 12

Brown Drake Nymph
Thread: Light brown
Tail: Three dark bronze hackles, trimmed and tied in.
Body: Tan with a grayish cast angora, or opossum.
Wings: Dark brown turkey
Hackle: Dark cree
Hook: Sizes 8 and 10

Brown Drake Spinner
Thread: Dark brown
Tail: Brown hackle fibers
Body: Yellowish brown poly, dubbed.
Wings: Gray poly yarn, tied spent.
Hook: Sizes 10 and 12

Cream Cahill (copies species like *Stenonema pulchellum* and
Stenonema modestum)
Thread: Cream
Tail: Cream hackle fibers
Body: Very pale cream (almost white) poly, dubbed.
Wings: Mallard flank feather dyed pale yellow, divided.
Hackle: Cream
Shuck (optional): Brownish black
Hook: Sizes 14 and 16

Cream Cahill Nymph
Thread: Olive brown
Tail: Light brown hackle fibers
Body: Dub pale creamish gray poly on the hook, and then tie pale brownish-
olive yarn in at the bend and bring it over the top to the wing case and tie in.
Wings: Dark brown turkey
Hackle: Dark olive brown
Hook: Sizes 14 and 16

The Cream Cahill looks a good deal like a Sulphur dun, and the hatches usually overlap.

Dark Green Drake (copies species like *Litobrancha recurvata*)
Thread: Dark gray
Tail: Dark brown moose mane
Body: Dark slate poly, dubbed and ribbed with yellow thread.
Wings: Mallard flank, heavily barred and dyed dark green.
Hackle: Rear, tannish brown hackle; front, dark brown hackle.
Shuck (optional): Tannish brown
Hook: Sizes 8 and 10

Green Drake (copies *Ephemera guttulata)*
Thread: Cream
Tail: Moose mane
Body: Cream poly, dubbed.
Wings: Mallard flank dyed yellowish green, divided.
Hackle: Rear, cream hackle; front, dark brown hackle
Shuck (optional): Pale grayish Z-lon
Hook: Sizes 8 and 10

Depending upon the quality of the hatch, you might tie Green Drake patterns as large as a size 6.

Green Drake Nymph
Thread: Tan
Tail: Three medium brown hackle, trimmed.
Body: Pale tan angora
Wings: Dark brown turkey, tied down and over thorax.
Hackle: Cree
Hook: Sizes 8 to 12

Coffin Fly (imitates Green Drake spinner)
Thread: White
Tail: Light tan deer hair
Body: White poly, dubbed.
Wings: Grayish yellow poly yarn, tied spent.
Hook: Sizes 8 and 10

Hendrickson and **Red Quill** (Hendrickson copies the female and Red Quill copies the male of *Ephemerella subvaria* and several closely related subspecies. In addition the Red Quill effectively imitates many *Ephemerella* spinners.)
Thread: Brown

Tail: Medium gray hackle fibers

Body: Red Quill—reddish brown hackle fiber stripped of its barbules and wound from the bed of the hook to the wings. Hendrickson—tan poly, dubbed.

Wings: Wood duck, divided. Hendrickson has gray hackle tips (optional).

Hackle: Medium gray hackle

Shuck (optional): Brownish-black Z-lon

Hook: Sizes 14 and 16

Hendrickson Nymph

Thread: Dark brown

Tail: Fibers from a mallard flank feather, dyed brown.

Body: Dark brownish-black angora, mixed with a bit of amber.

Wings: Mottled-brown turkey, tied down over thorax.

Hackle: Cree hackle

Hook: Sizes 12 and 14

Red Quill Spinner (Hendrickson)

Thread: Brown

Tail: Bronze dun hackle fibers

Body: Dark tannish brown poly, dubbed and ribbed finely with tan thread.

Wings: Pale gray poly yarn, tied spent.

Hook: Sizes 14 and 16

Light Cahill (copies many species)

Thread: Cream or tan

Tail: Cream hackle fibers

Body: Cream poly, fox fur, or angora, dubbed (for the female of *S. interpunctatum* the body should be cream-orange).

Wings: Mallard flank feather, dyed pale yellow, divided.

Hackle: Cream hackle

Shuck (optional): Dark brownish black

Hook: Size 14

Red Quill spinners imitate the male adult Hendrickson falling on the water in April and May.

Light Cahill Spinner

Same as dun except omit hackle and add pale yellow poly yarn for wings. Tie them spent.

Thread: Brown

Tail: Fibers from a mallard flank feather, dyed brown.

Body: Dark brown angora yarn on top and pale amber belly, dubbed.

Wings: Dark brown turkey

Hackle: Dark cree

Hook: Size 12

March Brown (copies *Stenonema vicarium*, now combined with *S. fuscum*)

Thread: Yellow

Tail: Dark brown hackle fibers

Body: Tan poly, dubbed and ribbed with dark brown thread.

Wings: Mallard flank feather, dyed yellowish-brown and divided.

Hackle: One cream and one dark brown, mixed.

Like many dun patterns, a nymphal shuck can be included as part of the March Brown dun.

Shuck (optional): Dark brown
Hook: Size 12

March Brown Nymph
Thread: Brown
Tail: Fibers from a mallard flank feather, dyed brown.
Body: Pale brown poly
Wings: Dark brown turkey, tied down over thorax.
Hackle: Dark cree
Hook: Size 12

Great Red Spinner (March Brown)
Thread: Dark brown
Tail: Dark brown hackle fibers
Body: Dark reddish brown poly, dubbed.
Wings: Pale gray poly yarn, tied spent.
Hackle: Dark brown with a turn or two of pale ginger, mixed.
Hook: Size 12

Little Blue-Winged Olive Dun (copies *Baetis tricaudatus*, and other members of the genus *Baetis*)
Thread: Dark gray
Tail: Medium to dark gray hackle fibers
Body: Gray muskrat or medium gray poly, dubbed; for the Little Blue-Winged Olive use olive-gray poly.
Wings: On smaller sizes (20) use dark gray mallard quills; on larger sizes use dark gray hackle tips.
Hackle: Blue dun
Shuck (optional): Brownish-black Z-lon
Hook: Sizes 18 and 20

Baetis Nymph (imitates Little Blue-Wing nymph)
Thread: Dark olive
Tail: Wood duck fibers, dyed dark olive.
Body: Dark olive brown opossum
Wings: Dark gray mallard quill section
Hackle: Cree or ginger variant hackle, dyed dark olive.
Hook: Size 18

Tying the Little Blue-Winged Olive dun will be a real test, as the various species this pattern imitates get as small as a size 20.

Rusty Spinner (Little Blue-Wing species)
Thread: Dark brown
Tail: Dark grayish brown hackle fibers
Body: Grayish brown poly, dubbed and ribbed with fine tan thread.
Wings: Pale gray poly yarn, tied spent.
Hook: Sizes 18 and 20

Slate Drake (copies all members of the genus *Isonychia*)
Thread: Black
Tail: Dark gray hackle fibers
Body: Peacock herl (not from eye), stripped; or dark gray poly, or muskrat,
dubbed.
Wings: Dark gray hackle tips
Hackle: One cream hackle tied in behind and one dark brown hackle tied
in front.
Shuck (optional): Black Z-lon
Hook: Sizes 12 and 14

Designed to ride high, the Slake Drake pattern copies a number of species.

Slate Drake Nymph
Thread: Dark brown
Tail: Three dark brown hackles with one side cut off.
Body: Dark brownish-black angora or opossum.
Wings: Dark gray mallard quill section, tied down over thorax.
Hackle: Cree hackle, dyed pale olive.
Hook: Sizes 10 and 12

White-Gloved Howdy (imitates Slate Drake spinner)
Thread: Dark brown or maroon
Tail: Medium gray hackle fibers
Body: Dark mahogany poly, dubbed.
Wings: Pale gray poly yarn
Hook: Sizes 12 and 14

Sulphur Dun (copies *Ephemerella rotunda, invaria, septentrionalis,* and to a lesser degree *dorothea*)
Thread: Yellow
Tail: Cream hackle fibers
Body: Usually pale yellow poly with an orange (sometimes olive-orange) cast (*E. septentrionalis* and *E. dorothea* have more yellow than orange in the body).
Wings: Pale gray hackle tips
Hackle: Cream hackle
Shuck (optional): Medium to dark brown Z-lon
Hook: Sizes 16 and 18

Sulphur Nymph
Thread: Grayish brown
Tail: Brown pheasant-tail fibers
Body: Brown (ground color) fur
Wings: Dark gray mallard quill section, tied down over thorax.
Hackle: Cree hackle
Hook: sizes 14–18

The Sulphur Emerger, with cream hackle (left) and the Comparadun (right).

Sulphur Spinner
Thread: Tan
Tail: Tan deer hair
Body: Female with eggs, yellowish tan poly; female without eggs, tan poly; male, bright red hackle stem, stripped and wound around hook.
Wings: Pale gray poly yarn, tied spent (also tie some upright).
Hook: Sizes 16 and 18

Trico Dun (copies all members of the genus *Tricorythodes*)
Thread: Pale olive
Tail: Cream hackle fibers
Body: Pale olive-green poly, dubbed; male, dark brown poly.
Wings: Pale gray hackle tips
Hackle: Cream hackle
Shuck (optional): Olive brown
Hook: Sizes 20 to 24

Trico Nymph
Thread: Black
Tail: Dark brown hackle fibers
Body: Dark brownish black fur
Wings: Dark gray mallard quill section
Hackle: Dark reddish brown
Hook: Size 22

Trico Spinner
Thread: Dark brown
Tail: Female, short cream hackle fibers; male, long, dark brown hackle fibers.
Body: Female, rear one-third is cream poly, dubbed, and front two-thirds is dark brown poly, dubbed; male, dark brown poly, dubbed, and ribbed with a fine, light tan thread.
Wings: White poly yarn, tied spent.
Hook: Sizes 20 to 24

The male Trico Spinner, one of the smallest patterns you'll need for limestone streams.

Yellow Drake (copies *Ephemera varia* and *Hexagenia rigida)*
Thread: Yellow
Tail: Tan deer hair
Body: Pale yellow poly, dubbed.
Wings: Mallard flank feather dyed pale yellow, divided.
Hackle: Pale yellow with a turn or two of grizzly in front.
Shuck (optional): Pale tannish gray Z-lon
Hook: Size 12

Yellow Drake Nymph
Thread: Tan
Tail: Pale gray, trimmed.
Body: Amber-colored angora or opossum
Wings: Medium to light brown turkey
Hackle: Ginger
Hook: Sizes 10 and 12

Yellow Drake Spinner
Thread: Yellow
Tail: Dark brown deer hair
Body: Pale yellow poly, dubbed.
Wings: Gray poly yarn, tied spent.
Hook: Size 12

White Mayfly (dun and spinner; the female dun never changes to a spinner, so this one pattern for both phases.)
Thread: White
Tail: White hackle fibers
Body: Female dun, creamish white poly, dubbed; male spinner, a couple turns of dark reddish brown poly at the rear, then white poly for the rest of the body, dubbed.
Wings: Pale gray hackle tips

The pattern for the White Mayfly can be used for both the dun and spinner because the female dun does not turn into a spinner.

Hackle: Cream (a turn or two of dark brown for the male spinner).
Shuck (optional): Pale tannish gray
Hook: Sizes 14 and 16

White Mayfly Nymph
Thread: Gray
Tail: Tannish gray hackle fibers
Body: Pale gray angora or opossum, dubbed heavily.
Wings: Pale gray mallard quill sections
Hackle: Cream ginger
Hook: Sizes 14 and 16

TWO TOP EMERGER PATTERNS

Emergers are an odd beast, neither nymph nor dun, and tying imitations for them is a bit different from anything else, so I've separated these two particular patterns from the rest. Both have proved highly productive for most of the hatches found on limestone streams. If the nymph is lighter then use the Pheasant Tail Emerger. If you want a darker body for the nymph then use the Turkey Tail Emerger. Add some weight to the shank of the hook to make the pattern sink.

Pheasant Tail Emerger (for Sulphur/Pale Morning Dun emergers)

Thread: Pale yellow

Tail: Tips of pheasant tail fibers

Body: Pheasant tail fibers wound around the shank and ribbed with fine gold wire.

Thorax: Fluff or after-shaft feather or the fine fuzz at the base of the pheasant tail, dubbed and wound around the shank two or three times.

Head: Make the head large and out of the yellow tying thread. To copy other mayflies use the general body color of the dun as the color of the head. For example, if you want to tie a Blue-Winged Olive Emerger then use dark olive thread for the enlarged head. For a Slate Drake, make the head from dark gray thread.

Hook: Nymph, size 14

Turkey Tail Emerger (for Blue-Winged Olive emergers)

Thread: Dark olive

Tail: Tips of turkey tail fibers

Body: Turkey tail fibers wound around the shank and ribbed with fine gold wire.

Thorax: Fluff or after-shaft feather or the fine fuzz at the base of the turkey tail or from an after-shaft of a feather from a saddle hackle, dubbed and wound around the shank two or three times.

Head: Make the head large and out of the olive tying thread. To copy other mayflies use the general body color of the dun as the color of the head. For a Blue-Winged Olive Emerger, use dark olive thread for the enlarged head. For a Slate Drake, make the head from dark gray thread.

Hook: Nymph, size 14

DOWN-WING PATTERNS: CADDISFLIES AND STONEFLIES

Down-winged imitations can bring trout to the surface on limestone streams. Prime among these down-winged hatches are the Grannom, Green Caddis, and Tan Caddis. All can create some fantastic dry-fly fishing on limestone streams. And don't overlook stoneflies on some of the faster stretches of limestone streams. Stoneflies don't seem to take on the significance of caddisflies, but in waters like Penns and Big Fishing Creeks, both in central Pennsylvania, these down-wings take on a high measure of importance.

Caddisfly Patterns

Caddis Nymph
Thread: Appropriate color (most often dark brown or black).
Tail: Olive, green, brown, yellow, black, or tan fur dubbed and ribbed with fine wire, or use a rubber band of the appropriate color and tie in at the bend of the hook and spiral to the eye.
Thorax: Dark brown fur, dubbed; or a dark brown (dyed) ostrich herl wound around the hook several times.
Hook: Sizes 12 to 18

Cream Caddis (copies some members of the genus *Hydropsyche*)
Thread: Tan
Body: Creamish tan poly, dubbed.
Wings: Medium brown deer hair
Hackle: Ginger
Hook: Size 14

Dark Blue Sedge (copies *Psilotreta frontalis*)
Thread: Dark gray
Body: Dark gray poly, dubbed.
Wings: Dark grayish brown deer hair

Hackle: Dark brownish black
Hook: Size 12

Emerging Caddis
Thread: Selected body color.
Body: Olive, green, brown, yellow, black, or tan fur or poly nymph-dubbing material.
Wings: Dark mallard quill sections, shorter than normal and tied in on both sides of the fly, not on top.
Legs: Dark brown grouse or woodcock neck feather wound around the hook two or three times.
Hook: Mustad 37160, sizes 12–18

Grannom (copies many species of the genus *Brachycentrus*)
Thread: Black
Body: Dark brownish black to black poly (with olive reflections), dubbed.
Wings: Dark brown deer hair
Hackle: Dark brown
Hook: Sizes 12 and 14

Green Caddis (copies many members of the genus *Rhyacophila*)
Thread: Green
Body: Medium olive-green poly with a gray cast, dubbed.
Wings: Medium brown deer hair tied in with butts pointing toward the bend of the hook and the tips of the deer hair extending out over the eye of the hook. Tie in hair securely near the eye of the hook, and then wind thread one-fourth of the way back towards the bend. Bend deer hair back and tie in.
Hackle: If you prefer the regular fluttering caddis, add a ginger hackle where you tie in the deer hair. Place a drop of lacquer on thread and finished head.
Hook: Sizes 14 and 16

This Black Caddis pattern has a shuck tied on to the hook bend to provide stability while it floats.

Little Black Caddis (copies *Chimarra atterima*)
Thread: Black
Body: Black poly, dubbed.
Wings: Deer hair dyed dark gray.
Hackle: Dark brown
Hook: Size 16

Spotted Sedge (copies *Symphitopsyche slossanae*)
Thread: Tan
Body: Grayish tan poly, dubbed.
Wings: Medium brown deer hair
Hackle: Ginger
Hook: Sizes 14 and 16

Stonefly Patterns

***Acroneuria* Nymph** (copies many species like *Acroneuria arida, abnormis,* and *carolinensis*)

Thread: Dark brown
Tail: Light brown hackle fibers
Body: Dark olive-brown yarn, laid over top of pale yellow dubbing fur.
Wings: Dark brown turkey
Hackle: Cree
Hook: Sizes 10 and 12

Early Brown Stonefly (copies species like *Strophopteryx fasciata*)
Thread: Yellow
Tail: Short, dark brown hackle fibers
Body: Dark grayish brown poly, dubbed; or peacock herl, stripped.
Wings: Dark brown deer hair
Hackle: Dark brown
Hook: Sizes 12 and 14

Early Brown Stonefly Nymph
Thread: Brown
Tail: Fibers from a brown pheasant tail

Between mayfly hatches, cast stonefly patterns; these insects emerge through the spring and summer.

Body: Reddish brown opossum dubbing
Wings: Brown turkey
Hackle: Brown
Hook: Size 12

Great Stonefly Nymph (copies many species like the common *Phasganophora capitata*)
Thread: Tan
Tail: Soft ginger hackle fibers
Body: Dark cream poly below with darker brown on top
Wings: Mottled turkey quill
Hackle: Cree
Hook: Sizes 8 and 10

Great Brown Stonefly (copies species similar to *Acroneuria lycorias*)
Thread: Dark brown
Tail: Short, dark brown hackle fibers
Body: Dark brownish gray poly, dubbed and ribbed with yellow thread.
Wings: Dark gray deer hair
Hackle: Dark brown
Hook: Sizes 10 and 12

Great Brown Stonefly Nymph
Thread: Brown
Tail: Light brown hackle fibers
Body: Light brown fur or nymph dubbing
Wings: Brown turkey
Hackle: Light brown
Hook: Size 10

Light Stonefly (copies species like *Isoperla signata*)
Thread: Pale yellow
Tail: Short ginger hackle fibers

Body: Pale yellow poly, dubbed and ribbed with tan thread.

Wings: Light tan to cream deer hair

Hackle: Ginger

Hook: Sizes 12 and 14

Light Stonefly Nymph

Thread: Tan

Tail: Fibers from a mallard flank feather, dyed brown.

Body: Tan fox fur or nymph dubbing

Wings: Light brown turkey

Hackle: Cree

Hook: Size 12

Yellow Sally (copies species like *Isoperla bilineata*)

Thread: Yellow

Tail: Short cream hackle fibers

Body: Pale yellow poly, dubbed.

Wings: Cream hackle tips, tied down-wing.

Hackle: Cree hackle

Hook: Sizes 14 and 16

PATTERN RECIPES FOR LIMESTONE STREAMS WHEN THERE IS NO HATCH

I often use the Patriot and the Trout Fin as the lead fly in a tandem rig when there is no hatch on limestone streams. Tie on one of the other patterns listed here as the dropper or "point" fly. This setup of using a dry fly and a wet fly is a deadly way to fish on limestone streams when there is no hatch, but it does work when there is a hatch in progress. Just use the pattern copying the dun for the lead fly and one copying a nymph or emerger for the point fly. Here are the patterns and recipes I most often use when I fish the tandem. In every wet fly but the Zebra Midge and the Brassie I add weight to the body before I tie the fly.

Dry Flies

Patriot

Thread: Bright orange-red

Tail: Brown hackle fibers

Body: Smolt-blue Krystal Flash wound around the shank. Wind some of
the red thread in the middle of the shank, similar to the Royal Coachman.

Wings: White calf-body hair, divided.

Hackle: Brown

Hook: Mustad 94833, size 10–18

Trout Fin

Thread: Orange

Tail: Brown hackle

Body: Orange floss

Wings: White calf-body hair, divided.

Hackle: Brown hackle

Hook: Mustad 94833, size 10–18

Fish the Patriot as the attractor dry fly in a tandem rig.

Why do trout strike an attractor fly like a Trout Fin? There's just something about it that agitates them.

Wet Flies

Bead Head Glo Bug

Thread: Red

Body. Two large strands of Glo Bug material in one of many yellow, blue, cream, pale orange, or orange colors. (I prefer the color they call "egg" and one dyed with Rit evening-blue dye.) Tie material on either side of hook, tie in with thread, pull tight, and tie just behind the bead.

Head: Copper bead

Hook: Tiemco 2457, sizes 12–18

Bead Head Olive Caddis

Thread: Olive

Body: Dubbed with a heavy amount of dark olive opossum fur, ribbed with fine gold wire.

Head: Copper bead

Hook: Tiemco 2457, sizes 12–16

In July and August the Bead Head Olive Caddis is a top producer, especially when fished as a dropper.

Bead Head Pheasant Tail

Thread: Dark brown

Tail: Five or six fibers from a ringneck pheasant tail

Body: Continue winding the pheasant tail fibers used to tie in the tail up to the bead, and tie in.

Thorax: Copper bead

Hackle: Ten pheasant tail fibers

Head: Copper bead

Hook: Tiemco 2457, size 12–16

Bead Head Tan Caddis

Thread: Tan

Body: Dubbed with a heavy amount of tan opossum fur, ribbed with fine gold wire. I tie several shades of this pattern.

Head: Copper bead

Hook: Tiemco 2457, sizes 12–16

The highly successful Bead Head Pheasant Tail imitates any number of species depending upon size and color.

Bead Head Woolly Bugger

Thread: Black

Tail: A mixture of black marabou and six strands of silver Flashabou

Body: Dark olive, gray, or black chenille palmered with a black saddle hackle.

Head: Copper bead

Hook: Mustad 3665A, sizes 10 and 12

Green Weenie

Body: Cut off a 5-inch piece of small or medium chartreuse chenille. Form a small loop with the chenille extending out over the bend of the hook, then wrap the chenille around the shank of the hook up to the eye.

Hook: Mustad 9672, size 10 or 12

Flashback Nymph

Thread: Brown or gray

Tail: Dark brown hackles

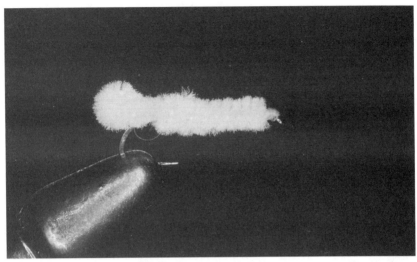

The Green Weenie is a sizeable hunk of food that trout grab, thinking it's some kind of grub or worm, or a very odd nymph.

Body: Tie some with a dark brown, black, and gray angora so you have a variety.

Thorax: Twenty to thirty strands of bright silver Krystal Flash or Flashabou tied in one-third of the way back from the eye. Pull the strands up over the eye and tie in. Make certain the strands cover the entire thorax, top and bottom.

Hook: Mustad 3906B, sizes 12–18

The Mink Thing (Created by Bob Toolan)

Thread: Dark brown, size 6/0

Body: Mink dubbed with guard hairs (add about ten wraps of 0.010 lead to the body before you add the mink.)

Head: Dark brown tying thread about twice as long as normal

Red Worm

Body: Cut a 5-inch piece of bright red chenille. Form a small loop with the chenille extending out over the bend of the hook, and then wrap the chenille around the shank of the hook up to the eye.

Hook: Mustad 9672, size 10 or 12

Midge Patterns

Al's Rat (Created by Al Miller)
Thread: Brown monocord
Body: Brown monocord
Thorax: muskrat
Hook: Size 20

Griffith's Gnat
Thread: Black
Body: Peacock herl
Hackle: Grizzly
Hook: Sizes 20–26

Gray, Black, or **Cream Midge**
Thread: Same as body color
Body: Gray, cream, or black
Hackle: Gray, cream, or black
Wings: Small pale gray hackle tips
Hackle: Dark gray, black, or cream (depending on body color).
Shuck (optional): Pale gray Z-lon
Hook: Sizes 20–26

Al's Rat, tied specifically for the trout in Little Lehigh Creek, has taken many a fish.

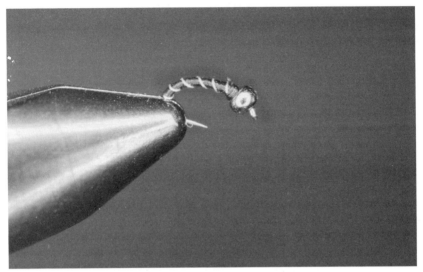

Never get caught without several Zebra Midges in your fly box—you can fish them anywhere, any style.

Red Brassie
Thread: Red
Body: Red wire
Thorax: Peacock herl wound two times around the shank just behind the eye.
Hook: Size 16–22 scud hook

Zebra Midge (pattern developed by Edward Welling)
Bead: Copper bead (brown body) or brass bead (black body)
Thread: Black or brown
Body: Use tying thread and make a very slim body with it.
Ribbing: Fine copper wire for brown and fine silver wire for black body
Hook: Size 16–20 scud hook

Scud Patterns

Scud Pattern #1
Thread: Dark olive, 8/0

Body: Tie in a half-inch-wide piece of clear plastic beyond the bend of the hook. After you form the body then pull this plastic up and over and tie it in at the eye.

Body: Dub in some dark olive seal.

Ribbing: Dark olive thread

Hook: Sizes 12–18

Scud Pattern #2

Thread: Tan, 8/0

Body: Tie in a half-inch-wide piece of clear plastic beyond the bend of the hook.

Body: Dub in some pink, amber, tan, or cream mohair or seal.

Ribbing: Fine gold or copper wire

Hook: Sizes 12–18

Simple Shrimp (Created by Mike Heck)

Thread: Medium olive, 6/0

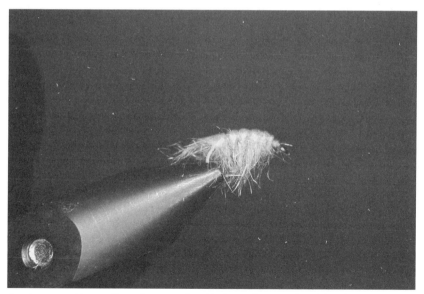

Scuds are another pattern that you should always have on hand just in case.

Tail: Partridge

Body: The dubbing is a blend of Orvis Spectra blend nymph, half olive and half light brown, and ribbed with silver wire. The back is brown Swiss straw.

Hook: Sizes 12–18

Cress Bug Patterns

Cress Bug

Thread: Dark brown, 6/0

Body: Use a dubbing loop and liberally dub dark olive brown imitation seal or Haretron. Use piece of Velcro to tease out the material. Trim on the top and the bottom and a bit on the sides.

Hook: Dai Riki 305, size 14 and 16

Kurt's Sow Bug (Created by Kurt Thomas)

Thread: Olive, tan, or gray, 6/0

Cress Bug patterns are very easy to tie; they don't have to be perfect.

Underbody: Dubbing, over wrapped with X-ray foil or other flat lead strip.

Body: Blend of fur or synthetic dubbing to match the natural

Hook: Mustad 3399

Terrestrial Patterns

Caterpillar

Thread: Black

Body: Black polycelon cut on the bottom and placed on the hook. Add quick-dry cement to hold to the shank.

Hackle: Tie in a grizzly saddle hackle at the bend of the hook and palmer up to the eye.

Hook: Size 10 or 12

Chernobyl Cricket

Body: Polycelon cut underneath with a slit and placed over the shank of the hook. Extend the body out past the bend half an inch. Add a drop or two of quick-drying cement to hold the body to the hook.

Wings: Tie in ten strands of deer hair, five strands of Krystal Flash, and a small piece of orange poly.

Hackle: Three black rubber legs on either side

Hook: Size 10

Ken's Hopper

Body: Yellowish olive, olive, or yellow poly, dubbed heavily.

Head and wings: Use deer hair dyed yellow and tie in just behind the eye as you would with the Muddler Minnow. Clip the butts also as in the Muddler.

Hook: Sizes 10–16

Letort Cricket

Body: Black poly, heavily dubbed.

Wings: Black-dyed goose quill sections, tied down-wing.

Hackle: Deer body hair, dyed black and tied in similar to the Muddler.

Hook: Sizes 12–16

Terrestrial patterns, especially larger ones like Ken's Hopper, are easy to see and follow on the water's surface.

Poly Ant

Body: Black poly, dubbed into two humps on the hook with the rear hump being a bit larger than the front.

Hackle: Add a black hackle after you complete the rear hump and before you start the front.

Hook: Size 12–20

Poly Beetle

Thread: Black poly yarn

Body: Tie in the poly securely below the bend of the hook. If you wish, tie in a peacock herl at the bend of the hook to imitate a Japanese beetle. Wind the tying thread up to the eye of the hook, and wind the peacock. Pull the poly up over the shank of the hook and tie in securely just behind the eye. Cut off the excess poly, but leave some to imitate the head.

Hook: Sizes 12–20

7

The Future for
Limestone Streams

The cool, consistent temperatures and alkaline buffer against acid rain are inherent qualities that help preserve limestone streams. But these streams face imminent troubles, and some waters have problems that might be irreversible. These threats materialize in two main ways: the degradation of the stream by farming and manufacturing, and privatization of the waters. Both threats are progressing at an ominous rate and both bode ill for the future of limestone streams and the general public.

By their very nature most limestone streams begin and flow in valleys that often hold valuable farmlands. The farmed lands often run right up to the bank of these streams. What is the effect of this? Little cover at the stream lets the sun heat up the water in the summer, and severe sedimentation problems ensue with a lack of cover. Chemicals used in farming and animal wastes create unwanted pollution. Cattle wading in the streams magnify the problem. All of these have a decided detrimental effect on the invertebrate and vertebrate life of the stream. Tests of limestone springs in Pennsylvania by the state and the Pennsylvania State University, in 1974 and 1985 respectively, show a marked increase in sodium, potassium, chlorides, nitrates, and fecal coliform bacteria. These are often associated with sewage disposal, highway deicing salt run-off, and agriculture.

Look at Penns Creek, a profound example of problems with upstream farming. Penns flows from Coburn downstream for miles through forest land. But above Coburn much of Penns Creek flows through heavily cultivated land. When the watershed receives a heavy dose of rain Penns flows chocolate brown for days and days. Even though the lower fifteen miles of this trout water holds little farming, the upper end has already created the damage.

Spring Creek in central Pennsylvania not only has farmland to cope with in its upper reaches, but also faces chemical effluents and sewage plants. These facilities have discharged pollutants into this fertile stream on more than one occasion. As a result, this once mighty insect factory now boasts only a few of its previous hatches. Years ago this fertile water held Green and Brown Drakes and dozens of other vital hatches. Now it holds only a few. Chemical pollutants were so prevalent in the early 1980s that the Pennsylvania Boat and Fish Commission stopped stocking trout in the stream. However, that continues to be one of the greatest positive decisions they have ever made. Within years a healthy population of stream-bred brown trout established themselves.

What can be done to prevent further pollution and continuous sedimentation events on some of our important limestone resources? We can encourage a buffer zone between the stream and tilled farmland. Land-grant universities, fish commissions, and other state agencies must work hand-in-hand to develop practical plans to prevent further erosion. One way to get immediate teamwork is through the pocketbook: If farmers actively cooperate in a conservation plan then they should get tax relief.

The other problem weighing heavy on limestone streams is privatization. This has occurred more quickly in the past few years for several reasons. First, private clubs have formed on many of these fertile waters. One landowner makes thousands of dollars when he provides cabins and fishing rights on a small limestone. Other nearby landowners see this whole process come to fruition and want to get in on a piece of the action. I've seen this trend spread in all directions. You cannot blame the landowner or farmer. For the farmer it's a quick and easy way to

This used to be the scene along Spring Creek—"No Trespassing"—but Pennsylvania purchased this section of the stream, creating access.

make some extra money that is not dependent on the shifting whims of weather.

What about hatcheries placed on many of these limestone streams? As I visited various streams for this book, I found that many of them held public and private trout hatcheries. These hatcheries add unwanted effluent to the streams below and should be monitored. Anglers and conservationists closed the hatchery operated by the Fish and Boat Commission at the head of Big Spring in south-central Pennsylvania several years ago.

How can we at least save some of our quality limestone streams for future generations? State agencies and fly-fishing organizations must become proactive immediately. Any bickering about what type of angler can fish what section of stream needs to be dropped in favor of joining forces and speaking with one voice. (Read about this in more detail in chapter 2, on Spring Run.) In Pennsylvania, as anglers take sides over fly-fishing-only versus artificials-only regulations, section after section of prime limestone water becomes private.

Cooperative efforts, such as this one on Potter Creek in southwestern Pennsylvania, are essential for the future of limestone streams.

First, let's guarantee access to some of our valuable waters no matter what method anglers use. If the state or some of the organizations have to pay an annual fee to keep some of these streams open, so be it. But we can't wait because privatization is advancing geometrically.

Four years ago I had a friend, Simon Grove, fish with me on Spring Creek in central Pennsylvania. Simon lives in London, England, and fishes a short stretch of private water one Friday afternoon each month. As we approached Spring Creek Simon continuously asked me if it was okay to trespass on the land.

"Are you sure it's all right with the landowner?" Simon asked.

Even when he entered the water he again asked me for assurance that he was doing nothing improper.

Is this how we want to go about our fishing—to suffer the same restricted access as our British counterparts? Unless we act now, within the next decade we will most definitely go the way of England.

This is not a matter of taking sides with the landowner or the angler. Taking sides means talks will remain at a standstill and the angler will eventually lose. Rather, the outcome has to be a win-win situation where both sides give something and get something. How can this happen? The landowner must gain something for his cooperation, either compensation in the form of an outright grant or tax relief on the property. Or how about creating a special state or federal stamp for access to these special limestone waters? The money collected would go to pay landowners on heavily fished waters, and would also cut down on the number of anglers. A stamp might also be used to encourage farmers to build a buffer between their farmland and the stream. State fish commissions must address this problem with a competent staff devoted just to access. How about adding a couple staff members for this and reducing a few from the propagation end?

There's another trouble looming on the horizon for limestones, and many other trout streams. Productive waters receive heavy angling pressure (and creates hard-to-catch trout). This angling pressure in turn creates posted land; property owners just don't like to see an army of rod-waving people marching all over their fields.

Virginia's Beaver Creek already benefits from limited-day access, which would aid other streams that get too much angling pressure.

Why not allow fishing only on a few days a week on some of the more crowded streams? That way landowners know what day anglers will be on the stream. If fishing on a stream is limited to Monday, Wednesday, and Saturday then the trout and the landowner get a break on the other four days. We already limit fishing on some of our better waters. The Massanutten Chapter of Trout Unlimited allows only four anglers per day on a two-mile stretch of Beaver Creek in Virginia. Parts of Cove Creek and Big Fishing Creek in central Pennsylvania are closed to Sunday fishing. The benefits of these measures are reduced access problems and less-pressured trout.

LITITZ RUN—A LIMESTONE STREAM HEADED IN THE RIGHT DIRECTION

Lititz Run begins its journey in center of Lititz, Pennsylvania. Much of its prime trout water flows through Amish and Mennonite farmland, and a good deal of this became eroded; the subsequent deposits produced an ailing, sediment-filled limestone stream. If Lititz were ever to become a vital, vibrant limestone trout fishery something had to be done quickly.

The revival of Lititz began harmlessly enough with a load of rock that Greg Wilson dumped at a site along Lititz Run that had been eroded by trampling cattle. Greg owned Woodland Concrete in nearby Bowmanstown, and that one inauspicious load of rock began a tremendous metamorphosis that ended with a totally renovated limestone stream.

Shortly after Greg dumped that load of rock along an eroded bank, that small section of stream began to improve drastically. Grass began to grow along the worn bank and this protected the stream from further sedimentation. The farmer who owned that section of stream noticed the improvement and was open to suggestions on further improvements by Greg and the Donegal Chapter of Trout Unlimited (donegaltu.org). Greg had asked for and received the backing of the local Trout Unlimited organization and its president that time, Bob Kutz.

With the organization now behind him, Greg approached other farmers along the stream and asked if they would cooperate allowing some major stream improvements. Greg, Bob, and Trout Unlimited worked upstream with each landowner until they completely renovated much of the bank along more than a mile and a half of the battered stream. They

Lititz Run, in Pennsylvania, is the scene of a terrific cooperative effort; the Creek Road section is the project of the Donegal TU chapter.

installed hog slats where cattle cross the water to prevent further sedimentation, added rocks to prevent bank erosion, and even removed an upstream dam. One obstinate landowner did not want them to touch his land so they bypassed it. Yet after that particular farmer saw the improvements to the other sections he revised himself and asked if the restoration team could renovate his section of the stream too.

Convincing the Millport Conservancy, Robert Wohlsen, and a wetland farm owned by John Banta at the upper end of the project to become a part of the renovation proved to be a difficult task. The dam on the conservancy land warmed the water below. Finally, Greg, Bob, and Trout Unlimited convinced the Conservancy to tear down the dam. That one decision helped cool the stream significantly and made the entire catch-and-release project a viable one.

But Greg, Bob, and the Donegal Chapter of Trout Unlimited were not alone in this project. Without the help of the landowners the project would never have come to fruition. Farmers like Marty Wenrich, Ed Hess, Art Hess, Wayne Brown, Robert Wenger, Jake King, and John King all should be congratulated for their tremendous cooperation. The Millport Conservancy, Robert Wohlsen, and John Banta also deserve accolades. A project such as this, which received the 2002 National Silver Trout Award from Trout Unlimited, also depended on other organizations for financial and moral support. Don Zimmerman, the Manheim Township Manager, Lititz Run Watershed Association, and the local Board of Supervisors helped ensure the success of this tremendous conservation project. Don't ever think that diverse groups can't or won't come together for conservation.

Lititz Run is now open to all. Visit the project along Creek Road just southeast of Lititz and fish it. It is a success that can and must be emulated elsewhere, because rescued or improved waterways improve land values and increase recreational economies.

OTHER PROMISING VENTURES

Lititz Run isn't the only stream headed in the right direction. Dozens of others have strong advocates working to improve stream conditions.

Stream restoration isn't just about fish—it's about trees, soil, water, wildlife, and an improved quality of life for residents.

Falling Spring Branch in south-central Pennsylvania has lost a great percentage of its once prominent hatches. Tricos and Sulphurs now appear in alarmingly decreasing numbers. The Falling Spring Greenway is trying to stabilize the situation.

The cooperation and diligent work efforts don't stop at the Mason-Dixon Line. What is presently happening to Beaver Creek in Maryland represents another splendid effort. Here the Beaver Creek Watershed Association has accepted the challenge and has shown great results. (Read more about the efforts of these organizations in chapter 3.)

Our quest to make limestone streams better and open to all anglers is a great one. The future looks somewhat brighter through the efforts of organizations presently working, and hopefully others will accept new challenges on other streams. We must, however, speak as one, and not fall into competing camps of spin fisherman versus fly fisherman versus bait fisherman. That's the quick way to lose. Anyone with a line in the water has a stake in the future.

SELECTED BIBLIOGRAPHY

Bashline, L. James. 1973. *Night Fishing for Trout.* Rockville Centre: Freshet Press.

Beck, Barry and Cathy. 2002. *Pennsylvania Blue-Ribbon Fly-Fishing Guide.* Portland: Frank Amato Publishing.

Brooks, Joe. *The Complete Book of Fly Fishing.* 1958. New York: A. S. Barnes.

Klots, Elsie B. 1966. *The New Field Book of Freshwater Life.* New York: G. P. Putnam's Sons.

Marinaro, Vincent C. 1970. *A Modern Dry-Fly Code.* New York: Crown Publishers.

Meck, Charles R., and Greg Hoover. 1992. *Great Rivers—Great Hatches.* Harrisburg: Stackpole Press.

——. *Trout Streams and Hatches of Pennsylvania.* 3d edition. 1999. Woodstock: Countryman Press.

——. *How to Catch More Trout.* 2001. Greenville: Beaver Pond Publishing.

——. *The Hatches Made Simple.* 2002. Woodstock: Countryman Press.

Needham, Paul R. 1969. *Trout Streams.* New York: Winchester Press.

MAP REFERENCE

Pennsylvania Geological Survey. 1990. *Limestone and dolomite distribution in Pennsylvania* (4th ed.): Pennsylvania Geological Survey, 4th ser. Map 15, scale 1:2,000,000.

ORGANIZATIONS INVOLVED IN RESTORATION AND PROTECTION OF LIMESTONE STREAMS

Maryland:
Beaver Creek Watershed Association
P.O. Box 207
Funkstown, MD 21734
www.bvrcrk.org

Pennsylvania:
Donegal Chapter of Trout Unlimited
P.O. Box 872
Brownstown, PA 17508
717-733-4939
www.donegaltu.org

Falling Spring Chapter of Trout Unlimited
Rod Cross
2670 Falling Spring Road
Chambersburg, PA 17201–9028
717-263-0365
www.fallingspringtu.com

Virginia:
Massanutten Chapter of Trout Unlimited
Dennis Patzig
1208 Windsor Road
Harrisonburg, Virginia 22801
www.massanuttentu.org

INDEX